Historic Dunfermline

THE SCOTTISH BURGH SURVEY

Historic Dunfermline

Archaeology and Development

E Patricia Dennison and **Simon Stronach**

Supported by
The National Lottery®
through the Heritage Lottery Fund

Carnegie Dunfermline Trust

Dunfermline Central Community Council

Dunfermline Historical Society

Published by Dunfermline Burgh Survey; Community Project

First published 2007

Copyright Dunfermline Burgh Survey; Community Project © 2007

E Patricia Dennison and Simon Stronach *have asserted their moral rights to be the joint authors of this work under the Copyright Act 1988.*

Dunfermline Burgh Survey; Community Project *acknowledges with gratitude contributions from the Heritage Lottery Fund, Historic Scotland, Fife Council, the Carnegie Dunfermline Trust, Dunfermline Historical Society and Dunfermline Central Community Council towards researching and publishing this volume.*

ISBN 978 0 9557244 0 4

Dunfermline Burgh Survey: Community Project
c/o Dunfermline Local Services Centre
Walmer Drive
Dunfermline
Fife
KY12 7JX

Edited by E Patricia Dennison

Publication management by SUAT Ltd

Design and typesetting by Christina Unwin

Printing and binding by Farquhar and Son, Perth

Front cover View of Dunfermline from the south, c. 1860. From MacDonald's
Tourist Guide to Aberdeen, Dundee and Central Scotland.
Courtesy of Bert McEwan

Contents

Figures

Plates

Abbreviations

APS — *The Acts of the Parliaments of Scotland*, eds T Thomson and C Innes (Edinburgh, 1814–75).

Cal. Docs Scot. — *Calendar of Documents relating to Scotland*, ed. J Bain (Edinburgh, 1881–8).

Chalmers, *Account* — *Historical and Statistical Account of Dunfermline* by P Chalmers (Edinburgh, 1884).

DES — *Discovery and Excavation in Scotland.*

DGCB — *Gild Court Book of Dunfermline, 1433–1597*, ed. E P Dennison Torrie (Scottish Record Society, 1986).

Dunf. Recs — *The Burgh Records of Dunfermline*, ed. E Beveridge (Edinburgh, 1917).

Dunf. Reg. — *Registrum de Dunfermelyn* (Bannatyne Club, 1842).

ER — *The Exchequer Rolls of Scotland*, eds J Stuart *et al* (Edinburgh, 1878–1908).

Henderson, *Annals* — *The Annals of Dunfermline and Vicinity*, by E Henderson (Glasgow, 1879).

NAS — National Archives of Scotland.

NLS — National Library of Scotland.

NMRS — National Monuments Record of Scotland.

NSA — *The New Statistical Account of Scotland* (Edinburgh, 1845).

OSA — *The Statistical Account of Scotland, 1791–1799*, ed. Sir John Sinclair. New Edition, eds I R Grant and D J Withrington (Wakefield, 1973).

PSAS — *Proceedings of the Society of Antiquaries of Scotland.*

RCAHMS — Royal Commission on the Ancient and Historical Monuments of Scotland.

RMS — *The Register of the Great Seal of Scotland, (Registrum Magni Sigilii Regum Scotorum)*, eds J M Thomson *et al.* (Edinburgh, 1882–1914).

RPC — *The Register of the Privy Council of Scotland*, eds J H Burton *et al* (Edinburgh, 1877–).

RRS — *Regesta Regum Scottorum 1153–1406*, eds G Barrow *et al* (Edinburgh, 1960–).

RSS — *Register of the Privy Seal of Scotland (Registrum Secreti Sigilli Regum Scotorum)*, eds M Livingstone *et al.* (Edinburgh, 1908–).

SBRS — Scottish Burgh Records Society.

Shearer, *Extracts* — *Extracts from the Burgh Records of Dunfermline in the Sixteenth and Seventeenth Centuries*, ed. A Shearer (Dunfermline Carnegie Trust, 1951).

SHS — Scottish History Society.

SUAT — Scottish Urban Archaeological Trust (SUAT Ltd).

TA — *Accounts of the Lord High Treasurer of Scotland*, eds T Dickson *et al.* (Edinburgh, 1877–1916).

TAFAJ — *Tayside and Fife Archaeological Journal.*

Acknowledgements

We are grateful to many people for their assistance in the production of this Dunfermline Burgh Survey.

The local history room, Dunfermline Carnegie Library, provided us with excellent facilities and unstinting good humour while dealing with our numerous requests. We would particularly like to thank Chris Neale, Dorothy Hall, Sharron McColl, Jeanette McMillan, Helen Penman and Catherine Pryde. The staff at the National Library of Scotland and the National Archives of Scotland were, as ever, extremely helpful. Staff at RCAHMS and Historic Scotland, in particular Richard Fawcett, Mark Watson, Peter Yeoman and Robin Evetts, gave most useful advice. We also benefited from the resources offered by the staff of Dunfermline Museums. To all of these we give our thanks.

We are indebted to the Guildry of Dunfermline for allowing access to some of their precious records; and we would also like to thank the Earl of Elgin for readily giving us access to his muniments.

Colleagues at Edinburgh University – Professor Bob Morris, Professor Michael Lynch, Professor Tom Devine, Dr Alex Murdoch and Dr Steve Boardman – kindly read our text and offered important advice. Douglas Speirs of Fife Archaeology Service, David Perry of SUAT Ltd and Dr Tim Holden of Headland Archaeology also gave support. Original illustrations were produced by Thomas Small and Linn Breslin of Headland Archaeology.

We would like to thank Dr Winifred Coutts for assistance with her palaeographic skills and Duncan McAra for his diligent copy-editing. We are grateful to those who loaned illustrations and photographs for reproduction (see figures list) and to the people in Dunfermline who kindly gave access to their properties. In particular we would like to thank Bill Fletcher.

Linda Steedman of eCom Scotland Ltd has given the project tremendous support with her website skills; and we would particularly like to thank her and the students of Lauder College, Dunfermline, for their assistance with a logo for this Community Project and the production of a website. SUAT Ltd have also been very supportive in the publishing of this Survey.

Most of all, the commitment and research efforts of the Community Project team have gone so much further than we had dreamed possible. As a result, this Survey cannot give full recognition to the wealth of information in the process of being discovered about this historic town. We would like to thank them all for their sterling support. In particular we mention Ronald Watt, chair of the project, Sheila Pitcairn, secretary, Jean Barclay, Alan Calder, Tobe Gardner, Bert

McEwan, Sue Mowat and Clive Willcocks, all of whom played very active roles and read and commented on our text. There were many involved in this project, as named below, as well as others who helped us on specific aspects of Dunfermline's historic and archaeological past. To all, we offer our gratitude.

Dunfermline Burgh Survey Community Project volunteers

Alison Anderson	Alan (Tobe) Gardner	Tom Minogue
Jacqueline Bain	Irene Gellan-Adams	Lizz Mogg
Anne Baker	Jim Gellan-Adams	Sue Mowat
Jean Barclay	Donald Gifford	Thomas Murphy
Gillian Baxter	Sandra Gilmour	Julie Orford
George Beattie	Rosalyn Hannah	Sheila Pitcairn
Bill Bedborough	Ann Harwood	Margaret Ritchie
Sheena Bedborough	Ann Hunter	Lynda Rudnicka
Jean Black	George Hunter	Muir Shaw
Sabina Black	Walter Hutchison	James Simpson
Olive Brown	Mary Johnston	Bob Smith
Louise Brugden	Mary Laird	Chris Sparling
Susan Buckham	Craig Lindsay	Linda Steedman
Alan Calder	George McBain	Simon Stronach
Ena Cochrane	Bert McEwan	Bob Tait
Winifred Coutts	Anne McIntyre	Jean Tait
Ken Cowe	Christine Mackie	Alison Thompson
John Crane	Bill Mackay	Karen Valentine
Jess Cumming	Sheila Mackay	Hugh Walker
Brian Dean	Greta Macpherson	Ann Watt
Pat Dennison	Joyce Matson	Ronald Watt
Lisa Dishart	John Mingay	Clive Willcocks
Audrey Ewing	John McNeely	Yvonne Willcocks

The third series of Burgh Surveys is intended to furnish local authorities, developers and residents with reliable information to help protect and manage the archaeology and historic environment of Scotland's urban centres. It acts also as a guide for the general reader to research the rich history and archaeology of Scotland's historic burghs. Although this Survey was produced in a different manner from the others in the series, that are published by Historic Scotland, it has similar objectives.

While there had been an earlier Burgh Survey of Dunfermline, it was much less detailed than those produced in the third series and had been restricted to secondary documentary sources. Also, it had been produced in the 1970s and, since that time, many changes have been made to the centre of the town and further redevelopment is now imminent or proposed. In view of this, local people invited Historic Scotland to produce a full-scale Burgh Survey in keeping with the standards of the third series. This was not possible in the light of the programme set by an advisory steering board and with so many burghs still awaiting an initial Survey.

Nevertheless, it was felt in Dunfermline that there was sufficient enthusiasm locally, and volunteers available to research some of the many records relating to the historic burgh and abbey, to seek supportive funding to produce an up-to-date Burgh Survey.

A Dunfermline Burgh Survey Community Project Management Group was set up to lead the project. Anchor funding was obtained from the Heritage Lottery Fund for the overall project and further supportive funding was provided by Fife Council and by Historic Scotland. Grants were also obtained for associated aspects of the project from Dunfermline Historical Society, Carnegie Dunfermline Trust and Central Dunfermline Community Council. Although the parentage of this Survey is different, this report, in consultation with Historic Scotland, follows the general format of the third series.

In its role as a tool for local authorities to use in the planning process, the first point of reference in this volume is the colour-coded town plan **plate 10**, which depicts the areas of prime archaeological interest. The general index gives rapid access to information specific to a site, street or feature within the burgh of Dunfermline.

Further preliminary research into the archaeological potential of a site within the historic town may be gleaned from local and national libraries and archives. The PASTMAP website (*http://www.PASTMAP.org.uk*) may also be consulted. This interactive website, supported jointly by Historic Scotland and The Royal Commission on the Ancient and Historical Monuments of Scotland, allows anyone with internet access to display and search data on Scotland's historic environment, including the legally protected sites – scheduled ancient monuments and listed buildings.

Both this Burgh Survey and the PASTMAP website provide information only. Where development is being considered, advice should be sought in all cases directly from Fife Council's Development Services and from the Council's Archaeological Unit (*see www.fifedirect.org.uk*).

Introduction

Medieval Dunfermline occupied south-facing slopes within walking distance – some three to four miles – of the Firth of Forth's northern coastline **figure 1**. Set on ridges running east to west, the upper and lower (or Nether) town, as is seen vividly on Blaeu's mid seventeenth-century map **figure 2**, seem to be almost separate settlements. To the north, the town was protected by marshy land – later called the 'Peel muir' – reflected today in the name 'Pilmuir'. The town was defined on the west by the steep slopes of Pittencrieff Glen, a valley carved out by Tower Burn **figure 3**. There have been various interpretations of the name 'Dunfermline' and no consensus has emerged.[1] It is agreed that the common Gaelic element 'Dun' indicates an early origin as a fortification. The Tower Burn was once called 'The Ferm' and Dunfermline may contain this former title and that of the Lyne Burn to the south, and suggest the former presence of a fort in the vicinity of these two watercourses.[2] Earlier historians tended to interpret the name as containing more descriptive elements, for example 'fort on the bend of the lynn' or indeed 'the watchfort by the rivulet'.[3]

1 Location of Dunfermline (Reproduced by permission of Ordnance Survey on behalf of HMSO. © Crown Copyright 2007. All rights reserved. Ordnance Survey Licence Number 100013329)

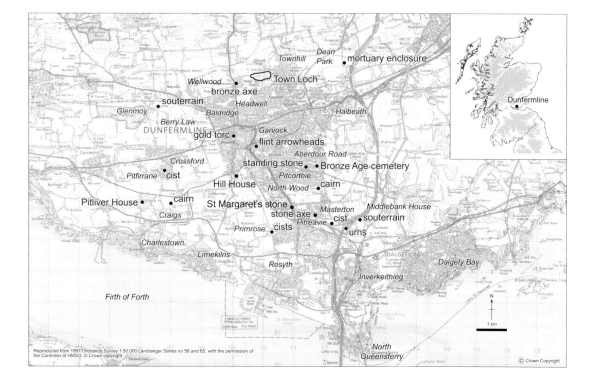

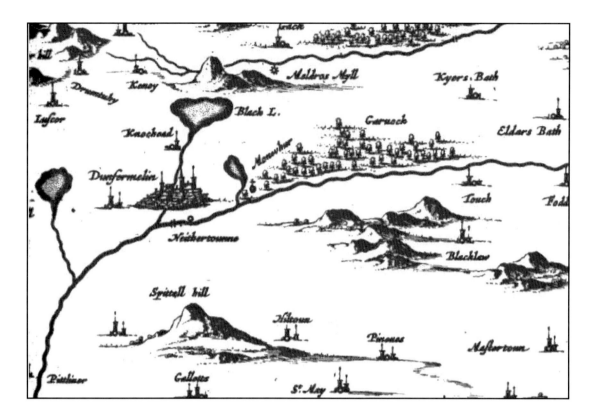

2 J Blaeu's Atlas,
View of Dunfermline,
Fifae Pars Occidentalis
(from T Pont)

An early reference to Dunfermline indicates it was the location
of the wedding between King Malcolm Canmore (1058–93) and
the Anglo-Hungarian princess Margaret in, or shortly after, 1067.[4] It
seems that there was already a church and royal residence associated
with the township,[5] and Queen Margaret then established another
small church (*see* p 16). With continuing royal patronage, the small
church developed into one of Scotland's most important monasteries.

Land use and geology

Dunfermline benefits from lying on the coastal fringe of Fife, which
is renowned for its fertile land. The underlying geology is formed from
Carboniferous limestone and sandstone that has developed into clays
and loams.[6] These rich soils and the mild climate, typical of Scotland's
east coast, combine to produce fine conditions for agriculture, and
this part of Fife has long been known for its productivity. A large
proportion of the surrounding farmland is devoted to arable crops
and traditionally most important have been cereals. This, in contrast
to Fife's less fertile interior, led to the much-quoted comment from
James VI (1567–1625) that Fife was 'a beggar's mantle fringed
with gold'.[7]

Economy

The medieval town's economy largely depended on servicing the
abbey and royal residence, and providing for the pilgrims who
came to visit the shrine of St Margaret, in the church, later abbey,
that she founded. The burgh acted as a market town for its rural
hinterland and benefited also from its central location between
the important centres of Perth, Stirling and Edinburgh.

   The economy of the town suffered when the Reformation brought
about the demise of the abbey but the associated royal palace complex
continued to be used as a royal residence. The Union of the Crowns
in 1603 with England, however, meant that royal connections with
the town became more tenuous, with a resulting impact on the burgh.

   In the eighteenth century the economy expanded, partly due to
the growth of coal mining, which had been undertaken on a small
scale from at least the medieval period when William de Oberville
granted the abbey the right to quarry for coal and stone in the lands
of Pittencrieff (*see* pp 38–9).[8] Linen weaving developed as a speciality

3 Aerial view
of Dunfermline
(© The Scotsman
Publications Ltd.
Licensor
www.scran.ac.uk)

of the town, and Dunfermline became the leading British manufacturer of table linen.[9] This declined during the twentieth century and all of the old factories have now closed.

Recently, new industries and employment opportunities, such as Sky, have been introduced, mainly on edge-of-town retail and business parks, which have led to moves to revitalise the historic core of the town.[10] The town's central location, particularly as a commuter-base to Edinburgh, however, continues to benefit its citizens.

Sources of information

Archaeological information concerning Dunfermline's past has come both from chance finds in and around the town and controlled excavations. The results from the more important excavations have been published in local and national archaeological journals.[11] Several smaller evaluations and watching briefs have also been undertaken and, although these may appear limited, the information retrieved is useful, especially when the results are synthesised. Reports of the work are held by RCAHMS, which also provides summaries in the online Canmore database.

Over the last century, aerial photography of the agricultural landscape around Dunfermline has identified a number of crop-marks, which are likely to indicate the locations of abandoned settlements such as souterrains at Glenmoy and Middlebank House **figure 1**, both protected as Scheduled Ancient Monuments. Only one modern excavation has been undertaken on a prehistoric site in or immediately around Dunfermline and our knowledge of the area is likely to grow considerably with each new archaeological excavation.[12]

A Burgh Survey of the town was published in 1978, but the historical research was based solely on secondary sources. The Dunfermline Burgh Survey Archaeological Update supplemented this in 1998 and included information from archaeological projects undertaken since the first survey.[13] A discussion of the town in the light of the many excavations that have taken place since 1978 has been completed relatively recently.[14] There are many publications concerning the justifiably famous abbey and palace complex.[15] Local people have always been proud of the heritage of Dunfermline, and several excellent publications concerning varied facets of the town's past have been produced.[16]

Dunfermline has a wealth of primary sources that offer insights into its past. Many of these have been accessed for this Survey, as noted in the Bibliography. There are, however, still pockets of documentary sources that would benefit from further research. The Burgh Court and Council records have not been studied in their entirety, particularly those of the nineteenth century. Dunfermline is fortunate in having the earliest extant guild court records in Scotland, starting in 1433. These have been assessed up to the eighteenth century only. Nineteenth-century newspapers have not been fully trawled; nor has time allowed a full assessment of the records of local industries. The records of the linen and silk manufactories and more recent works, such as the Globe Bottling Company, which bottled Maclay's Oatmeal Stout in Woodhead Street (Chalmers Street), Gilbert Rae's aerated water and Woodrow's mineral water businesses, could possibly give a deeper understanding of the town and its economic evolution. Rosyth Dockyard has had a huge impact on the development of Dunfermline in the twentieth century. No papers relating to the yard have been assessed in this exercise. All of these would merit research if a still greater understanding of this historic town is to be gained.

RCAHMS also holds information on many of the buildings in the town and this may be supplemented from published sources.[17] This includes a large collection of photographs, which can be used to establish the form of the townscape prior to modern development, and records of buildings now lost such as the Opera House.

Representations of the town in historic maps are also an important source of information. The town is shown on a manuscript created by John Gordon in 1642, probably based on the work of Timothy Pont (*c*.1590s), and on a version of the same plan published in 1654 by Johann Blaeu, although they do not show any detail. The first map to do so was produced by William Roy between 1747 and 1755 **plate 1**.[18] In even greater detail is John Wood's plan of 1823 **figure 4**.[19] Ordnance Survey town plans surveyed in the second half of the nineteenth century also provide much useful information.[20] The National Library of Scotland maintains a website from which these early plans may be easily accessed. Less easily available are manuscript maps, and several early examples were discovered in Dunfermline Carnegie Library, Local History Room, during the course of the Survey.[21] Copies of early engravings, such as those by J Slezer, and paintings are also very useful in helping to gain an understanding of the historic town; some are held in the collections of RCAHMS but others are less accessible and remain in private collections.

Listed buildings and scheduled ancient monuments

Dunfermline Abbey and Palace, the Heugh Mills, Malcolm Canmore's Tower, the Nether Yett, a stretch of precinct wall on Canmore Street and St Catherine's Chapel and Almshouse are designated Scheduled Ancient Monuments, meaning that the archaeological remains within them and their setting have been given statutory protection by Scottish Ministers.[22] A little outside

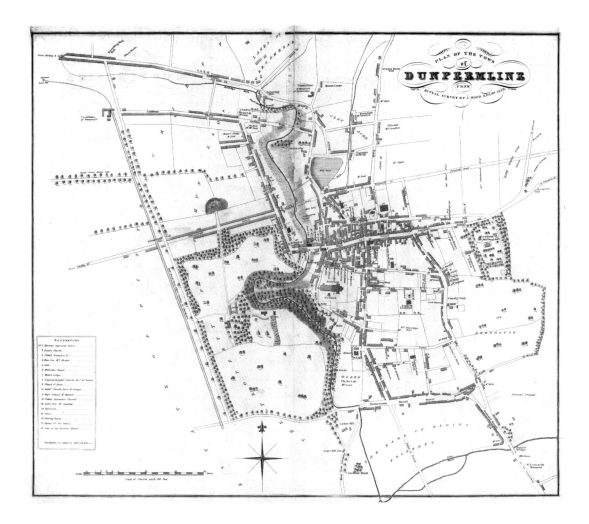

4 John Wood's plan
of Dunfermline, 1823
(Reproduced by
permission of the
Trustees of the National
Library of Scotland)

the medieval town, but within it today, Perdieus Mount is also
a Scheduled Ancient Monument.[23] Some of the Scheduled
Monuments are also Properties in the Care of Scottish Ministers
acting through their agency Historic Scotland.

Over 140 buildings in Dunfermline are listed by Scottish Ministers
as Buildings of Historic or Architectural Interest. The list is
maintained by Historic Scotland.

The medieval core of Dunfermline lies within a designated
Conservation Area. This means that the area has been determined by
the local authority to have a special architectural or historic interest,
the character of which it will seek to preserve or enhance.[24]

The archaeology of the area before the town emerged

Prehistory

Studies have shown that the area would once have been covered with
forest and by about 3,000 years ago much of Fife appears to have
been cleared, probably because of both climate change and human
action.[25] Now only isolated pockets of woodland survive in areas
that were too steep or marginal for agriculture.

The earliest evidence for settlement around Dunfermline dates
to the Neolithic period and includes chance finds of a stone axe and
some flint arrowheads **figure 1**.[26] More unusual was an elaborately
carved stone ball found near the town.[27] More substantial evidence
for Neolithic activity may survive near the town at Deanpark House
figure 1 where a cropmark has been interpreted as a possible mortuary
enclosure.[28]

Much more evidence dating to the Bronze Age has been uncovered
and this leaves an impression that even by this early stage the area
was assuming some importance. Several spectacular finds, including
a bronze axe found in Wellwood and a gold torc from the parish
churchyard **figure 1**, have been reported over the years.[29] Discoveries
of Bronze Age burials in cists have been reported from Crossford and
Masterton.[30] The latter was the most impressive and contained a pair
of armlets, a bronze dagger and a jet necklace. These are thought to
have accompanied a double burial with both bodies apparently laid
on the hide of a European bison.[31] The most recent excavation of
Bronze Age remains was undertaken at Aberdour Road **figure 5**.[32]
This was a cemetery containing at least six burials. Some were

5 Prehistoric urns
(We are grateful to the
Society of Antiquaries of
Scotland for permission to
reproduce these images)

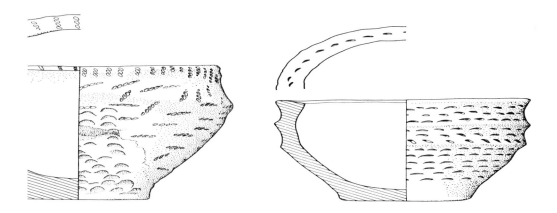

interments in short cists while other bodies had been cremated. A small group of cists was also recorded on Primrose Farm, to the south of the town.[33] An early account of the discovery of 'Roman urns', also likely to have been Bronze Age cremations, can be added to this rich record.[34]

Two cairns, also probably associated with burials, have been noted in the vicinity. One survives at North Wood, while no trace of the other at Craigs Farm remains **figure 1**.[35] Perhaps the most tangible upstanding monument from this time is the standing stone at Pitcorthie.[36] Although now isolated and somewhat incongruous in the midst of a housing estate, this stone may not have moved far from its original position and the name of the area is likely to derive from it.[37]

The later prehistoric period is poorly represented in the area, in stark contrast to the regular discovery of Bronze Age remains. There are two possible settlement sites in the vicinity, at Glenmoy and Middlebank House **figure 1**, which are thought to include souterrains and may date to the Iron Age or subsequent period.[38]

Roman period

Fife was part of the territory belonging to a tribe the Romans called the Venicones.[39] There are some Roman sites in Fife but compared to other parts of the country these are scarce.[40] They amount to only tantalising evidence of the extent of Roman military activity.[41] It is altogether unclear what strategy the Romans pursued with regard to the inhabitants of Fife or indeed whether relations were openly hostile.[42] There is common agreement that, at the very least, the Roman fleet would have been familiar with the Fife coastline and a feature likely to be the mouth of the River Eden is shown on Ptolemy's map made in the second century AD.[43] It is without doubt that the presence of the Romans must have impacted on the people who lived in the Dunfermline area. At the very least they must have been able to see a Roman fort across the Forth at Cramond on a clear day.

Dark Ages

As is well evidenced by the analysis of place-names, and the nature of archaeological sites, Fife was part of what archaeologists refer to as 'Pictland', which ran from the Forth to the Beauly Firth.[44] Some references by Roman and later historians suggest that the residents were variously called the Maeatae, possibly the Pictish Verturiones, and finally the Southern Picts.[45] However, there is no firm historical intelligence concerning the area during this period and we have only a very general level of knowledge. After the Northumbrian Angles had taken over Lothian in the seventh century AD the Forth represented the frontier between them and the Picts and the area around Dunfermline must have been strategically vital. Place-names, including Dunfermline itself, suggest that by the ninth century the area was becoming part of the spreading Gaelic-speaking Kingdom of the Scots (*see* p 15).[46]

In the immediate vicinity of Dunfermline there is perhaps a surprising paucity of finds dating from this period. The most evocative reminder of the Picts is the frequent occurrence of names beginning with 'Pit' and, when analysed collectively, these suggest that there may have been a site of some importance in the area.[47]

The town today

Dunfermline has spread far beyond its medieval limits and much of this has occurred over the last century. The scale of this expansion can readily be seen by looking at the modern map compared to Wood's made in 1823 **figures 1 and 4**. Expansion to the west has been prevented by Pittencrieff Park but has extended as far as Wellwood in the north, Halbeath and to the M90 in the east and Pitcorthie and Masterton to the south.

For the purposes of this study the town has been divided into four areas, as shown in **plate 10**:
  i Pittencrieff Glen and west of Tower Burn;
 ii north of the abbey precinct;
iii New Row and Netherton;
iv the abbey precinct.

Notes

1 For a full and recent discussion see S Taylor with G Markus, *The Place-Names of Fife: Volume 1 West Fife between Leven and Forth* (Donington, 2006), 308–11.

2 S Taylor, 'Welcome to Fothrif', *Scottish Place Name Society Newsletter*, 13 (Autumn 2002).

3 P Chalmers, *Historical and Statistical Account of Dunfermline* (Dunfermline, 1844), i, 2–3; J Fernie, *A History of the Town and Parish of Dunfermline* (Dunfermline, 1815), 2.

4 Fordun, Johannis de, *Chronica Gentis Scotorum*, ed. W F Skene (Glasgow, 1871–2), liber v, 213.

5 *Dunf. Reg.*, no 1.

6 J B Whittow, *Geology and Scenery in Scotland* (London, 1977), 124.

7 J Gifford (ed.), *The Buildings of Scotland: Fife* (London, 1988), 19.

8 *Dunf. Reg.*, no 323.

9 Gifford, *Buildings*, 175.

10 'Royal Dunfermline: a City Awakening' – prospectus of the 'Royal Dunfermline' project.

11 Recent examples include R Coleman, 'Excavations at the Abbot's House, Maygate, Dunfermline', *TAFAJ*, 2 (1996), 70–112; and J Lewis, 'Excavations at the former Lauder Technical College, Dunfermline', *PSAS*, 125 (1995), 1023–44.

12 J Close-Brooks, M Norgate and J N G Ritchie, 'A Bronze Age cemetery at Aberdour Road, Dunfermline, Fife', *PSAS*, 104 (1971–2), 121–36.

13 R Gourlay and A Turner, *Historic Dunfermline: the archaeological implications of development* (Scottish Burgh Survey, 1978); SUAT *Historic Dunfermline; the archaeological implications of development* (Scottish Burgh Survey Update, 1998).

14 D Perry, 'Dunfermline: from "Saracen" castle to "populous manufacturing royal burrow"', *PSAS*, 129 (1999), 779–816.

15 The most recent being: R Fawcett (ed.), *Royal Dunfermline* (Edinburgh, 2005).

16 For example, S Pitcairn, *A History of The Old 'Fitpaths' and Streets of Dunfermline, Then and Now* (Dunfermline, nd); and B McEwan, *Dunfermline: Our Heritage* (Dunfermline, 1998). For fascinating accounts concerning aspects of the town's industrial heritage see H Walker, *Dunfermline Linen: The History of Hay & Robertson Ltd and the Robertson Family of Dunfermline* (Dunfermline, 1996) and H Walker, *The Story of Erskine Beveridge and St Leonard's Works, 1833–1989* (Dunfermline, 1991).

17 For example, see Gifford, *Buildings*.

18 W Roy 1747–55, *Military Survey of Scotland*, British Library Shelfmark: Maps C.9.b.17.10/1.

19 *Plan of the town of Dunfermline from actual survey* by J Wood of Edinburgh 1823 (Wood 1823).

20 Ordnance Survey 1856, *Town Plan of Dunfermline*, Sheets 1–7, Surveyed 1855, Scale 1:1056; Ordnance Survey 1896, *Town Plan of Dunfermline*, Sheets XXXVIII.4.20, 4.24, 4.25, 8.5, 8.10 and XXXIX 1.21, 1.22, Surveyed 1894, Scale 1:500.

21 'A View of the Town of Dunfermline, with the situation and distance of the [—] from the said town, surveyed and delineated in the year 1766 by [—]' (1766 map), in Dunfermline Carnegie Library, Local History Room; Hunt & Welwood, *Plan of Heugh Mills of Dunfermline with Mill Dams & Mill Leads Belonging Therein* (1836, manuscript map held in Carnegie Library Local History Department).

22 *NMRS* NT 08 NE 01, 02, 08 and 94.

23 *NMRS* NT 08 NE 30.

24 Historic Scotland, *Memorandum of Guidance on Listed Buildings and Conservation Areas* (Edinburgh, 1998).

25 C Gillen, 'Rocks and Landscapes', in *The Fife Book*, ed. D Omand (Edinburgh, 2000), 9.

26 *NMRS* NT 08 NE 83 and NT 08 SW 17.

27 D N Marshall, 'Carved stone balls', *PSAS*, 108 (1976–7), 43.

28 *NMRS* NT 18 NW 25.

29 *NMRS* NT 08 NT 37 and J J Taylor, *Bronze Age Goldwork of the British Isles* (Cambridge, 1980), 91.

30 *NMRS* NT 08 NE 36 and NT 18 SW 33.

31 *NMRS* NT 18 SW 33.

32 Close-Brooks, 'Bronze Age cemetery', 121–36.

33 J G Callander and T H Bryce, 'Bronze Age short cists near Dunfermline, Fife. With a report on the bones found', *PSAS* lvii (1922–3), 299–302.

34 *NMRS* NT 18 SW 14.

35 *NMRS* NT 08 NE 22 and NT 18 NW 12.

36 *NMRS* NT 18 NW 4.

37 S Taylor, 'Some early Scottish place-names and Queen Margaret', *Scottish Language*, 13 (1994), 1–17.

38 *NMRS* NT 08 NE 38 and NT 18 SW 116.

39 E Proudfoot, 'Living with the Romans', in *The Fife Book*, ed. D Omand (Edinburgh, 2000), 35–43.

40 G S Maxwell and J N G Ritchie, 'Prehistoric, Roman and Pictish Fife', in *Buildings*, ed. Gifford, 26–7.

41 Maxwell and Ritchie, 'Prehistoric', 26–7.

42 Proudfoot, 'Living', 40, or for an alternative view, Maxwell and Ritchie, 'Prehistoric', 26–7.

43 Maxwell and Ritchie, 'Prehistoric', 26.

44 Taylor, 'Welcome to Forthrif'.

45 Maxwell and Ritchie, 'Prehistoric', 27.

46 S Taylor, 'Place-names of Fife', in *The Fife Book* ed. D Omand (Edinburgh, 2000), 209.

47 Taylor, 'Queen Margaret', 4–7.

6 Dunfermline's burgh seal, showing Malcolm Canmore's Tower (from E Henderson)

Dunfermline in the Middle Ages

The site of early Dunfermline

Dunfermline enters the historical scene in the eleventh century. According to the fourteenth-century chronicler John of Fordun, King Malcolm Canmore married the Anglo-Hungarian princess Margaret, daughter of Saxon Edward who had been exiled in Hungary, some time between 1068 and 1070 at a place called Dunfermline.[1] Described as an 'oppidum', it is not clear whether this means a settlement or a fortified place. What has also puzzled many is exactly where this place was. Tradition has it that the so-called Malcolm Canmore's Tower in Pittencrieff Glen **figures 6 and 34** was the site of the king's hunting lodge and the dwelling of the king and queen. Certainly, such a location would be highly defensible, surrounded as it was within a loop of the Tower Burn and its steep ravine – an important factor in the choice of royal residence – and offering easy access to the wooded policies of Pittencrieff, and beyond, for hunting.

An alternative first settlement site has at times been suggested – somewhere in Pittencrieff Park. The reasoning behind this view was that David I (1124–53) referred to his burgh of Dunfermline as being *citra aquam*.[2] If 'citra' is used as a preposition, the meaning would be 'Dunfermline on this side of the water (or 'nearer side of the water') in which the monastery is situated'. (*see* p 3 for further discussion).

If the name 'Dunfermline' is considered, however, another alternative site may be implied (*see* chapter 2). It includes the common Gaelic element 'Dun', which suggests a fortification. It also makes reference to a burn once called 'The Ferm' – now named Tower Burn – and the Lyne Burn to the south.[3] The town's name suggests an early origin as a fortification in the vicinity of these two watercourses. But Malcolm Canmore's Tower is not close to the Lyne Burn. Might it be possible that the first settlement at Dunfermline was further south, close to the two burns – perhaps in the region of Perdieus Mount **plate 10**? It is certainly very unusual to have both an upper and a 'nether' town – as seen so vividly in J Blaeu's mid seventeenth-century view of Dunfermline **figure 2**. If the first settlement was in the Netherton region, the creation of 'New Row', so called from at least the fifteenth century, skirting the eastern boundary of the Benedictine monastic precincts, was an essential routeway giving access from the original settlement to the market town north of the abbey.

It is known also from Fordun that there was already in existence a small church nearby; and this may have been a further reason for attracting Malcolm Canmore to the Dunfermline area. The small church was possibly on the same site that the queen established a new church; and local tradition, based on a reference in Dunfermline's chartulary, argues that the masons who worked on this lived at the village of Masterton **figure 1**.[4] It was of sufficient importance to receive extensive grants from King Malcolm.[5] Favoured by both the king and Queen Margaret, their sons, Alexander I (1107–24) and, in particular David I, would transform it into one of the most prestigious abbeys in the country.[6] The abbey complex in effect divided the upper and lower townships **figure 4**. Settlement would be expected to cluster at the gate of an important abbey or cathedral – as, for example at Elgin, Coupar-Angus, Melrose and Arbroath. But it is very unusual to have a township on both sides of a large monastic complex. This topographical factor may also support the theory that the original Dunfermline was in the Netherton area, which later moved its nucleus further north.

Dunfermline becomes a burgh

It is known that Dunfermline had become a royal burgh some time between 1124 and 1127, if not earlier. During this time David I granted to the church dedicated to the Holy Trinity *unam mansuram in burgo meo de Dunfermlyn* – 'a house or dwelling place in my burgh of Dunfermline'.[7] The church had been founded by his parents, possibly on the site of the little pre-existing early church. Receipt of burghal status brought both privileges and obligations, the most important privileges being for a freeman to hold property and attend the town's market without payment of toll, or duty. The obligations included attendance at the three annual burgh head courts and defence of the town. Along with these, there was a formalisation of the urban setting, with the laying out of streets and burgage plots, or tofts, where the privileged inhabitants – the burgesses – would build their homes. Who this early planner was is unknown. He may have been a skilled monk from the Church of Holy Trinity which David I had elevated to an abbey but, whoever he was, the town plan fitted admirably into the natural setting of geography and geology.

The town plan

Dunfermline sits on a series of ridges running from east to west, formed by glacial drifts in prehistoric times. Between the ridges there was clay soil which tended to be water-retentive and peaty. These ridges gave not only protection from high winds, but also a spring-line

fed the town from the watery peat muir to the north.[8] This was to be a hilly town – Netherton Broad Street stands at approximately 51 m above sea level, the present Priory Lane lies at 69 to 67 m west to east, 90 to 101 m at the High Street west to east, and on a line from Bruce Street up Queen Anne Street the lie is 92 to 105/106 m. This means, in all, a rise from south to north of some 55 m.

There are few early descriptions of the town. Some time between 1350 and 1424 Andrew of Wyntoun wrote that Dunfermline was 'a lytill hill of nobill ayre, all wode about both thick and fayre', stressing not only the woodedness of the area, but also its steepness and royal presence.[9] French lords and knights lodged in the town in 1385. The Valenciennes-born Jean Froissart stressed the smallness of the town,[10] but it must have been considered of some significance to receive such prestigious visitors.

By the time burghal documentation is extant in the fifteenth century, it is clear that the townspeople had adapted ingeniously to the natural setting. The main street **figures 7 and 8** – Causagait, Hiegait or Mercatgait – ran along one of the ridges, conveniently supplied with the spring-line from the muir to the north. A back lane, Rotten Row,

7 left High Street of Dunfermline, nineteenth century (from a postcard, the Wrench Series, courtesy of Bert McEwan)

8 right High Street, 2006 (courtesy of Bert McEwan)

Backside and Sculgait, lay to the northerly rear of the tofts on the main street and another lane, variously called In Below the Wa's, In Between the Wa's or the Foul Vennel, served the same function to the south. This southerly back lane gained its rather unpretentious names as it was a little lane running between the small back walls or fences of the tofts aligned on the south side of Causagait and the high abbey precinct wall. It is now known with some certainty from archaeological research that this lane once joined up with Maygate and in all probability gave access also to the New Row. The vennel is now hidden below the present Canmore Street, such has been the accumulation of debris since the Middle Ages, but it may still be entered from cellars on the south side of the street. Collier Row, Cross Wynd and Sculwynd gave access to the north of the town, with a routeway leading from the west end of the main street called 'the common road leading to the cemetery' or Maygate – the same name as that of the adjoining road running west to east. This 'common road leading to the cemetery' would later be called St Catherine's Wynd and gave access to the parish church, the nave of the abbey **figure 34**, as well as to the churchyard and cemetery, and was the main exit from the town to the west. Cross Wynd's west side was developed in 1489; John Wright, who owned property fronting onto High Street, sold off this land, thus releasing it for the laying out of tofts on the west side of the wynd.[11]

To the south of this medieval settlement the abbey complex formed a vast mass of building and open space dividing the upper from the 'nether' town **plate 1**. The townspeople were largely excluded, apart from those lay people who worked in the abbey, such as kitchen staff, plumbers, washer-women and garden odd-job boys.[12] The one area where the townspeople might enter was to their parish church, which was the nave of the conventual church, and the churchyard and cemetery to the north. This parish church was often called the 'wtyr' church; that is, it was considered to be without the conventual precinct (the conventual church being sometimes referred to as the 'inner' kirk).[13] It survives today to the west of the present Abbey Church, although much changed in the interior since the Reformation (*see* pp 29–30). The abbey lands were bounded to the east by the properties on the 'calsay' – called New Row **figure 9** since at least the fifteenth century – the routeway giving the important access by the Spittal Bridge **figure 10a** to Queensferry. In the 'nether' town the Common Vennel, once known as the Abbot's Coach Road and now Priory Lane, marked the limits of the abbatial complex, and running parallel was the broad street called the Netherton. Turning south from here, past Perdieus Mount, was the main route to Limekilns, Wester Gellet and Rosyth, a vital access to landlocked Dunfermline's port **figure 1**.

9 New Row, showing
calender house
on the left
(from D Thomson)

The built environment

Although Dunfermline had close links with its rural hinterland, it
was visually set apart from the country. Important urban buildings
and other physical features made it different from a village, even
though there were probably only a few hundred people in the town.
One of the most distinctive statements was the erection of gates or
ports (in Scots – yetts). They were designed both to exclude outsiders
and the unwanted and also to allow access to the town's market,
where tolls were collected from those who came to buy and sell. The
gates were closed at dusk when the curfew was called and opened at
dawn – usually 5 a.m. in summer and 6 a.m. in winter. The town had
a number of ports to monitor both entrance and exit **figures 34** and
35. The West Port, at St Catherine's Wynd **figure 11** is documented as
early as 1328.[14] The steep approach road over the gyrth bow through
the Pittencrieff policies is shown on Slezer's late seventeenth-century
engraving **figure 12**. The East Yett stood at the east end of High Street
and is still remembered in the name 'East Port'. At the north end of
Collier Row was a further port, often called the Mill Port **figure 13**,
due to the mill that stood in the vicinity (*see* p 24). A 'new yett' north
of Causagait is documented in 1490 and nine years later a 'new port
of the Cross Wynde' is recorded. This may well have been built
specifically to help keep plague out of the town.[15]

Gates into the town might seem to imply walls round the town,
but this seems not to have been the case initially. The majority of
Scottish medieval towns were merely surrounded, at most, with a
ditch and a wooden palisading fence. Normally the fencing relied on
the individual burgesses who placed fences at their 'heid dykes' at the

10a Spittal Bridge and St Leonard's Works (courtesy of RCAHMS; © Crown Copyright: RCAHMS; Erskine Beveridge Collection)

b Looking eastwards from possible weavers' houses at Buffies Brae over the railway viaduct to St Margaret's and Pilmuir Works (courtesy of Mark Watson)

end of their tofts. Often these fences were punctuated with small gates giving access to the town's common lands. So, they were clearly not defensible, but rather psychological markers defining the town proper and the countryside beyond. When Edward I of England (1272–1307) occupied the town in 1303–04 he instructed that a ditch should be built to encircle the town, which rather suggests that there was until this date no substantial demarcating ditch.[16] Whether his instructions were carried out in full or part is not clear. The fact that a dwelling was built at his command 'extra magnam portam abbacie de Dunfermlyn' ('outwith the great gate of the abbey of Dunfermline') shows that certain building works were effected.[17] There is little other evidence of walling or ditching until the fifteenth century. Plague was prevalent in 1445 and the records indicate that a wall was built to

11 West Port and
St Catherine's Wynd
(by E Henderson;
courtesy of Dunfermline
Carnegie Museum)

counteract infection.[18] This may have been a wooden structure,
because in 1503 seven burgesses were instructed to take down the
wall at Rotten Row and replace it with stone.[19]

The most important physical symbols of the town's prestige and
authority were the parish church and the tolbooth. Some sense of the
grandeur of the parish church may still be witnessed in the imposing
extant medieval nave – the original parish church – of the new Abbey
Church. What has been lost is the atmosphere that the altars and all
their rich accoutrements gave to the church, as well as the sumptuous
decoration which would have adorned the walls and pillars. The
townspeople had no access to the canons' choir and presbytery, which
occupied the eastern limb, on the site of the present Abbey Church,
reportedly 'becomingly furnished with books and ornaments and

12 J Slezer's 'Prospectus Oppidi et Caenoby Fermelodunensis', *Theatrum Scotiae*, the view from the north-west

13 The Mill Port (from D Thomson)

other ecclesiastical jewels' and deemed 'one of the major cultural centres of late fifteenth-century Scotland'.[20] This eastern conventual church was completed sometime before 1250; until that time it was probably the place of worship for both laymen and monastics, but thereafter the nave became exclusively a parochial church.[21] Yet, there would have been an impact on the lay people of the canons' choir and presbytery. The townspeople cared for the furnishings of their parish church, such as stone and wood carvings, paintings, rich vestments, bejewelled crosses and candelabra.[22] The records also make it very clear that the town, by its collection of 'lycht sylver', ensured that there was always an adequate supply of candles to light the altars in the parish church.[23] The primary documentation also shows that by the end of the fifteenth century there was a high altar

and at least six others – dedicated to the Rood and Our Lady, St Margaret, St Nicholas, St Ninian, St Salvator and the Holy Blood.[24] Adjacent to the monastery wall to the north was sited the prestigious dwelling of the abbots **figures 14 and 15**, now known as Abbot House (*see* pp 27, 34 and 82).

The abbey attracted many pilgrims to it, their main purpose being to visit the shrine of St Margaret. Fragments of the chapel, which was added to the east of the conventual church for the shrine of St Margaret shortly before 1250, may still be seen to the east of the modern Abbey Church. Dunfermline became one of the foremost centres of Scottish pilgrimage; and even as early as the twelfth century the scale of the abbey building reflected the importance of what had already become the mausoleum of the royal house of Scotland, with David I's parents and six brothers all already buried in the church.[25] It was in the abbey complex that Edward I resided from November 1303 until February 1304. Clearly, the accommodation was worthy of royalty. On the departure of the English army fire destroyed many of the buildings. Matthew of Westminster's account says that the conflagration was extensive, 'sparing from the flames the church only and a few lodgings for monks'. It was here, however, that the son of Robert I (1306–29) was born, so it would appear that by this time the accommodation had been sufficiently repaired and upgraded as to be fit for the queen and her household. The choice of Dunfermline for the location of his tomb is sure indication that the king held Dunfermline Abbey in reverence.[26]

The tolbooth was the lay symbol of the town's authority. This, too, was maintained by the townspeople. It stood at the west end of Causagait, facing up the street. Its function was to act as a repository for the tolls paid by those who came to the market, so the town weights

14 Abbot House from the north (from P Chalmers)

15 Abbot House in 2006, showing part of the City Chambers

were deposited here; it housed both the burgh court, the guild court[27] and at times the regality court, the normal meeting place for the last probably being in the chapter house of the abbey. It also acted as the local jail and the town's stocks were, in consequence, held in the tolbooth when not in use.[28] Being of great significance in the town, it was probably at least in part built of stone. The records show that the roof was slated – an unusual feature in the town, most buildings being thatched (*see* p 27) – but this did mean that, in spite of the innovation, the town had to maintain the roof on a regular basis.[29]

Dunfermline's geology determined that, unlike many market towns, such as Montrose and Inverkeithing, there was no open market space. Dunfermline's market had of necessity to be linear, stretching the full length of Causagait, and even beyond the East Port[30] – an important indicator of the economic importance of medieval Dunfermline. The town's weighing machine – the tron – stood in front of the tolbooth but the market cross, probably because of congestion, was, unusually, at a small distance from the tolbooth – at the foot of Cross Wynd.

The townspeople also maintained other strategic features of the town – the roads and the water supply. Side streets, vennels and pathways, if surfaced at all, were probably covered in wattle and timber. The main streets may have been cobbled or paved. Causagait seems to have been upgraded to this state at least by 1477, when paving stones, gutter stones and sand were purchased and a 'Michael caswamaker' came to advise on this process.[31] It is also possible that the important route to the port at Limekilns was also partially paved or cobbled. In 1438, William Gelland (Gellet) was admitted to Dunfermline's guild merchant at a reduced fee of ten shillings off the usual 40 shilling entrance sum for 'his gud dedis doand till the makyin of a casway betwiyx the lym kill and our ton of Dunfermlyn'.[32]

Being a town situated on ridges, water control and supply was, from the outset, a vital aspect of town organisation. The earliest documentary evidence shows that the town, probably influenced by the Benedictine monks, harnessed water by a series of communicating channels. Water from the Town Loch, sometimes called Moncur, to the north of Dunfermline **figure 1**, was led to the Abbey Mill Dam, from which it then fed a mill at the top of Collier Row. At this point it was flagged over as a culvert, passing, according to contemporary documentation, to the rear of the properties at the west side of the street and round the back of the tolbooth, before passing into Maygate and the abbey lands.[33]

Almshouses, chapels and schools

The town had two almshouses. That dedicated to St Catherine
stood near the abbey. The first mention of St Catherine's Chapel
and eleemosynary house occurs in a charter of the abbey in 1327.[34]
The chapel was possibly demolished by December 1420,[35] but
remnants of the almshouse survived the Reformation[36] and may
still be seen in St Catherine's Wynd **figure 16** (*see* p 117). There was
another almshouse just outside the East Port, on the north side.
It is not known who supported this.[37]

   To the south of the town on the route to North Queensferry were
the hospital and chapel of St Leonard **plate 2**. Tradition has stated
that it was founded by Malcolm Canmore and Queen Margaret; in
the Register of St Leonard's Hospital in 1651 it is noted that the
almshouse and chapel of St Leonard were founded in the reign of
Malcolm Canmore.[38] A more likely possibility is that it was founded
by a later Queen Margaret, the wife of Alexander III (1249–86),
when many other St Leonard hospitals were established.[39] It may
have been at one point a leper hospital. Henryson's poem 'The
Testament of Cresseid' alludes to this by its siting of a leper house.
What is known is that the hospital supported eight widows who
were each supplied with a chamber and donations of meal, malt,
wheat and groats harvested from the 64 acres of land adjacent to
the hospital. They were also given eight loads of coal a year and
some also received a pension of two shillings of silver.[40] The Spittal
Lands are shown clearly on a map in the Elgin Archives, sitting to the
east of the Guild Lands, a clear indication of the reliance of the town
on its rural hinterland in the Middle Ages.[41]

16 Remains of St Catherine's
Chapel and Almshouse
(courtesy of Bert McEwan)

At the south-west of Netherton, probably at a site at the head of the present Elgin Street, was St Mary's Chapel **plate 10**.[42] Saint Ninian's Chapel was founded in the early years of the sixteenth century to the east of Collier Row[43] – on a site now vulnerable to proposed development. A mile or so to the east of the burgh, at Garvock, was St John's Chapel.[44]

The town had two schools – a song school intended largely to train choristers for the abbey[45] and a grammar school. There may also have been a third by 1525.[46] A burgh sasine of 1496 sites the grammar school at the north-east corner of Rotten Row at the top of 'the commone gait extendand to the Gramour Scull', later called the Sculgait.[47]

The homes of the townspeople

An integral part of the town plan was the laying out of burgage plots. One of the obligations of a burgess was that his plot should be 'biggit' – or built on. To assist the earliest burgesses a period of time – known as the 'kirseth' and usually one year and a day – was given free of burghal taxes, to enable them to build their properties. This was a policy that continued, in a different format, throughout the Middle Ages. The town authorities raised money from developed land through taxation. If due payment were not made 'recognition' or forfeiture of the plot resulted. If a plot was not built on and payments fell into arrears there was little to forfeit. The Dunfermline burgesses were, therefore, regularly prodded to make their plots 'strainable by bigging'.[48]

The tofts ran at right angles back from the streets. Liners, burgh officers, were appointed to ensure that all respected their allotted space, the frontages all being carefully measured. The liners, in their role of overseeing the built fabric of the town, also dealt with such matters as checking that one property did not make its neighbour less watertight. They decided when there was dispute who should pay for mutual walls, brought action when the eaves of one house was dripping into the neighbour's burgage plot and oversaw, along with a bailie, the resignation and receipt of exchange of tofts by the traditional method of 'erde and stane'. This meant that a forkful of land was physically handed over as a symbol of exchange of land.[49]

It is clear also from the contemporary records that each dwelling had the theoretical right to 'lights' and was not to be blocked by another house. Few of the windows offering light would have been glazed; at night-time shutters closed the window space and some, by day, may have been covered with a light canvas material.[50]

Lengths back from the frontage varied enormously. Those on the north side of Netherton, running all the way back to the Common

Vennel (now Priory Lane) were the largest. But, in spite of this, properties in the Maygate, Causagait (High Street) and west side of Collier Row were the most desirable, as they were close to the two most important built features of the town – the parish church and tolbooth. Collier Row was, however, a narrow street – until 1770 it was only 12 feet (3.7 metres) wide at its south end. It was widened when Bridge Street was built (*see* p 41) and in consequence the original frontages at the south end of the street were forward by eight feet (2.5 metres) to those at present. It probably takes its name from the Gaelic word 'coille' – a wood or forest.[51] New Row was less heavily developed **figure 9**, the east side having a few houses but also several crofts and agricultural lands. On the west, the plots ran hard up to the monastery wall.[52]

Most burgesses chose to build their homes at the front of the toft. Initially, these were probably very simple wooden structures, sometimes of only one room. But by the time the burgh records are extant in the fifteenth century there are references to lofts, cellars, forestairs, vaults and forehouses – which implies increasing sophistication in the style of housing.[53] Most would, however, still be of wood, some possibly having a ground floor of stone. The traditional roofing was thatch of either heather or turf, probably cut from the Peel Muir, or water-resistant growing plants. Peat and wood were probably the most common fuels for heating the homes, but coal was abundant in the Dunfermline region, so may have been in more common use than in other towns. The guild house was certainly heated with coal by 1503.[54] Slated roofs were an innovation. There was a slater, John Kelly, resident in the town in 1497 and a Robin Sklatter had worked on the tolbooth.[55] This seems to imply that there were a few slated buildings providing opportunity for work. But the records speak specifically of the 'sclait house' on the 'kirkyard dyk'.[56] To use this phrase is to suggest its unusualness. This may be a reference to Abbot House. In 1490, it was occupied by John Orok, one of the town's bailies.[57] The only other mention of a slated house comes in 1506[58] – west of the tolbooth and inhabited by John Moffat (Montefixo), the schoolmaster, so it is possible that his predecessor – Robert Henryson – schoolmaster and poet – lived here also. His poems would suggest this was the case. In all probability both properties were owned by the church, which could afford such prestigious roofing; and it is known that in 1468 Richard de Bothwell, abbot, provided a house for the schoolmaster.[59]

Being a market, the Causagait was lined with wooden booths attached to the front of the houses, where the local craftsmen might display their wares.[60] These temporary structures in time became permanent, so lessening the width of the main street. In the backlands of the tofts, residents kept their animals, sunk their wells and dug their midden pits. In time, however, the business premises of tradesmen occupied this rear land – there is evidence of kilns, bakehouses, smithies, brewhouses, barns and forges.[61] As a result, particularly in sought-after areas such as Causagait, the infilling of the back-lands – a process called repletion – with buildings to the rear of the principal dwelling, gave rise to closes giving free 'ische and entrie' (exit and entry).

Terra Communis – the common lands

The burgh muir to the north of the town was used by the burgesses to pasture animals, as well as being a source of both fodder and roofing material. The common muir stretched approximately from the lands of Baldridge to the neighbourhood of Townhill, being a gift of the abbot to the burgh in return for an annual payment of 6d sterling.[62] The muir was assiduously protected from encroachments by unfreemen. In 1549, for example, one Edward Elder was to 'tak tent to the common muyr and se gif the nolt herd keip the samyn fra ai unfremen withtout the burgh and to schaw the balyeis gif ony takis haddir turf or paitis of the same and girs'.[63] The burgh marches were perambulated – either on foot or horse – every year to ensure that there had been no encroachments.[64]

At Netherton was another piece of land of importance to the townspeople – the butts.[65] Here, shooting practice took place and this was probably also the venue for 'wappenschaws', when the burgesses were obliged to bring out their weapons as evidence that they could defend their town in time of danger.

Social control in the Middle Ages

Deviant behaviour within the community was frowned upon, since this affected the status quo of burgh life. Punishments in the town highlight the perceived nature of crimes – they were offences against society. For this reason, most offences were atoned by public humiliation. The stocks sat outside the tolbooth, when in use, so that all could come to mock and hurl rubbish at their offending neighbour. Or a culprit might be placed at the 'jougs' – an iron attachment that went round the neck, normally attached to the tolbooth wall – again for public display. Women might be placed in the cukstool and ducked in water; quite where this was is uncertain. Some unfortunates might even have their ear nailed to the tron, so that, yet again, they were subjected to public ridicule. Fines were also imposed, usually being put to church work. More serious offences met with imprisonment in the tolbooth; but the most severe of all was banishment from the town for a period of time or for good after branding on the cheek.[66] One further feature of punishment in Dunfermline was the 'lear stane'.

Exactly where this was sited is unknown, but it would probably have been in a public place near the tolbooth. This was used to deal with the offence of 'detraction' (slander). It seems to have been disliked by certain members of the community: it disappeared and had to be replaced in 1499.[67]

Dunfermline in the sixteenth and seventeenth centuries

Street pattern

The street pattern of Dunfermline, laid down in the Middle Ages, remained virtually unchanged for the next two centuries – indeed, it is possible to this day to trace the medieval core of the town through the alignment of roads.[68] What was to change radically in this time were the buildings. This was largely due to three main factors: the Reformation and its impact on the abbey; the departure of the crown and court to England in 1603; and the disastrous fire of 1624 which virtually wiped out the central core of the town.

The Reformation and the town

There is little or no evidence to show that the Protestant Reformation was welcomed by the townspeople. With their close ties to the abbey, the 'old order' underpinned the town's livelihood and very existence. It made for a conservative cast of mind, likely to view change and disruption with suspicion well beyond the Reformation of 1560. The sixteenth century had seen the control of the abbey passing into the hands of commendators who, like Archbishop Beaton of St Andrews and his nephew, George Dury, who succeeded him, were probably for the most part non-resident.[69] The monks remained in residence. Records make it clear that the guild merchant feared the arrival of the Protestant Lords of the Congregation who were in retreat through Fife, pursued by French troops, in 1559.[70] As a result of this impending danger, the pertinents of the Holy Blood Altar had to be divided up for safekeeping since the people of Dunfermline lived in a 'troublous world'.[71]

But the Reformation came. Some thought this was not a permanent situation. The feuar of the abbey's almonry lands entered into an agreement in 1598 with provisos that, in the event of the Reformation being overturned, alternative arrangements would be made.[72] Exactly what destruction was perpetrated, the records do not make fully clear. Certainly, altars and their rich pertinents would have been desecrated, although some altars in the abbey church and also a number of monks survived until well into the 1580s.[73] It is thought that the choir, or inner, church suffered more than the nave, or parish church, but even the inner church could not have been largely destroyed if some of the monks were able to bar themselves in their church in 1580 to keep watch over the shrines of St Margaret and King David and the sepulchre of Robert Bruce.[74] In the parish church the north-west tower, now the site of the steeple, was damaged, taking with it part of the west gable, when the bells within, which had been 'baptised,' came under attack.[75]

The records of the Privy Council in 1563 suggest that the physical damage done by the Reformers in 1559–60 was compounded in the following three years by neglect.[76] But the damage to the church fabric was possibly not such as to prevent some worship continuing in the building, although reparation work was effected in 1564 and again from 1570.[77] In 1572 a pension was provided for the abbey slater, which suggests that roofing had been repaired.[78] With the coming of the Reformed Church much of the abbey's extensive lands were resigned and set in feu to lay people,[79] as were the yard and dovecot of St Catherine's Chapel in 1566.[80] By 1587, the temporalities of the abbey, with a few exceptions, had been transferred to the crown but, significantly, the Benedictine monks were to be allowed to enjoy their pensions, livings and places of residence throughout their lifetimes.[81] As late as 1605 funds were still being set aside for monks and nuns.[82]

As well as being sited beside a prestigious abbey, the town also benefited from the presence of royalty. Around 1540 the royal palace appears to have been repaired and enlarged. Large mullioned windows were added to the existing structure and an extra floor with both mullioned and bay windows overlooking the Glen **figure 12**, still to be seen today, was added.[83] There was to be an even greater royal presence in the reign of James VI. On the day after his marriage to Anne of Denmark at Oslo in Norway in 1589, the king presented her with a 'morning gift' of one of the royal houses at Dunfermline. £400 was given to the master of works, William Schaw, to upgrade the property prior to her arrival. The following year, the queen was granted the lordship of Dunfermline, and by 1594 had taken formal possession of it.[84]

Queen Anne liked to reside in Dunfermline. A new house was built for her, probably on the same site as the original granted to her, close to the abbey and palace.[85] Views of the queen's house suggest it was three-storeyed **figure 11 and plate 3**. It had a pend running under it leading to the palatial courtyard.[86] It was in Dunfermline that the Princess Elizabeth was born in 1596, the future King Charles I (1625–49) in 1600 and the following year Prince Robert. The palace and the queen's house made this a highly desirable area in which to live. Added to this, in 1599 two large residences were built close to the old church steeple, for the high constable and the heritable bailie of the regality.

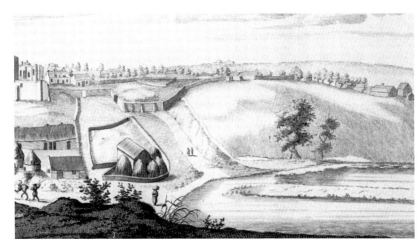

17 J Slezer's 'Prospectus Caenoby Fermelodunensis', *Theatrum Scotiae*, view of Dunfermline from the south

It was thanks to Queen Anne and the king that repair works were effected on the abbey. With the act of annexation of the abbey pertinents and the queen's position, holding the lordship of Dunfermline, the commendatorship of Dunfermline Abbey was resigned by Henry Pitcairn, the last commendator, to the queen. Renovation of the abbey began in 1593 with William Schaw as King's Master of Works. The state of the church before repair is unclear, but there had been an appeal to the king in 1588 to intercede for its repair, which would suggest deterioration since the repairs of 1564 and after.[87] Work was relatively extensive and lasted some five years. A new steeple adorned the bell tower, the fifteenth-century porch at the north door was extended, the upper part of the west gable was taken down and rebuilt and some buttresses were added to the north and south gables. The interior was also refurbished. Ongoing works meant further improvements. Nave renovations continued until 1607; the town council, however, was concerned that the new renovations to the roof were being undermined by locals climbing up onto the roof, purportedly to plunder crow and dove nests, but in reality stealing lead and slates.[88] A royal gallery was erected in front of the pulpit for the accommodation of the royal family, when in Dunfermline, in 1610.[89] The front of the gallery may be seen in the new Abbey Church on the north wall of the north transept, beneath the stained glass window. In spite of these improvements, the south aisle of the nave was showing signs of decay in 1620 and a further buttress had to be added to the south wall.[90]

The departure of the Crown to London

It was probably with some sadness that the townspeople witnessed the departure of the royal family to London in 1603 when James VI succeeded to the throne of England. Although Dunfermline was not a permanent royal residence there were strong links with the town. The magnificent palace was left to the charge of Lord Seton, tutor to Charles I, and Henry Wardlaw of Balmule, the chamberlain. In 1616 the royal burial vault, situated between the south-east buttresses and possibly first used when the little Prince Robert was interred in 1602, was now no longer of use to the royal family. It was gifted to Henry Wardlaw, as may still be seen on the stone inscription above the door. Dunfermline was not totally forgotten, however. In 1610 the queen mortified £2,000 Scots to provide salaries for the masters of the grammar and music schools.[91] The following year she had constructed a new bridge over the Tower or Ferme Burn **figure 18**, probably on the site of the medieval gyrth bow. Above the arch were the initials 'A R'

18 Double arch over Tower Burn in 2007

(*Anna Regina*) and the date 1611 (*see* p 32).[92] But it was not until 1617 that the king returned, and then briefly, although work on the palace had been undertaken in view of this visit.[93]

In spite of the departure of the crown and many of the nobility attendant at court, Dunfermline, in certain areas, remained a prestigious place to live; and it is known that three important houses were built in the early part of the seventeenth century. Around 1610, Pittencrieff House **plate 3** was constructed for Sir Alexander Clerk of Penicuik.[94] His armorial insignia and initials may still be seen over the door. In 1621 a house of two storeys, with vaulted ground floor, was built on the north side of East Netherton Street **figure 19**. On the ground floor there was a huge fireplace, with a fine iron grate; attached were various appliances for use by a cook. It is thought that the grate was of such quality that it might have come from the abbey or palace. From probably around 1790, when manuscript volumes of the regality court and various charters were discovered in the attic, it was called Regality House.[95] It was demolished in 1861. Hill House, still extant to the south of Netherton on the road to Limekilns **figure 1**, was built for William Monteith of Randieford in 1623. The initials 'W M' are engraved above the window at the main entrance.[96]

The townscape

Plague threatened Dunfermline, as many other towns, fairly frequently. The town council took measures to ensure the safety of the town, denying movement in and out of the town when plague was prevalent,[97] Queen Margaret, wife of James IV (1488–1513) herself being forced to stay in the town due to 'pestilence' in 1504.[98]

19 View of old Netherton
(from D Thomson)

In 1584–5 Dunfermline rid itself of the infection more quickly than other towns and, for this reason, it was chosen as the only safe meeting place for parliament. As was becoming the practice, the General Assembly of the Church of Scotland was to convene ahead of parliament, but on arriving on 23 November all the town gates were shut and the clergy refused entry. The provost, the laird of Pitfirrane, said this had been done on the express command of the king.[99] Whether or not this was the case, it is sure evidence that the town ports were being carefully maintained, probably having been made extra secure in the time of plague to bar outsiders who might bring in the infection. That they continued to be looked after is clear when in 1606 the locks of both Collier Row Port and East Port were mended.[100] Three years later, when plague hit Burntisland, the townspeople were forbidden to entertain others from outwith the burgh, for fear of the town becoming infected.[101]

Other pre-Reformation features of the townscape remained. Below the monastery wall, the dovecot in St Lawrence Yard **plate 4** and the grain mill at Collier Row were still standing – and functioning – in 1632.[102] Supply of water to them, however, was dependent on the continuing careful management of the Moncur Loch and the Mill Dams, which at times was deemed to be negligent.[103]

Other features of the town needed maintenance – the tolbooth and tron were always regular drains on the town's finance; and the town clock was taken apart, repaired and cleaned in 1605 at a cost of seven shillings.[104] The market cross by 1620 had become so dilapidated that the town council took the decision to remove and replace it. The model for the new cross copied closely Edinburgh's and Aberdeen's extant crosses, although smaller. It had an octagonal base which could be entered by a door, with a pillar atop crowned with a unicorn.[105] This pillar had to be replaced in 1695.[106] This shaft is now located in the garden of Abbot House, having been yet again replaced in 1992. St Margaret's Stone **figure 1**, where by tradition Queen Margaret had rested on her journey into Dunfermline, was maintained on the main route from North Queensferry to Dunfermline.[107]

It is clear that council officials continued to keep control of the built fabric of the town and did not allow unlicensed construction work. Two men needed specific permission from the council to build malt kilns in front of their barns in the Backside (Queen Anne Street now) in 1607.[108] It is possible that Rotten Row Port was re-erected about this time, having certainly been in existence in the late sixteenth century.[109] Sanitation was an ongoing issue – middens and closets were forbidden on the main streets – and the townspeople were not to wash their clothes in the lade that led from the Town Loch.[110] This essential water supply to the town was constantly supervised by the town council.[111] The records also make it clear that the land associated with many of the properties in Netherton were still extensive, some having crofts and orchards.[112]

Fire

Much of this built fabric of the town was destroyed in a disastrous fire in 1624. The 25 May was Dunfermline's 'wappenschaw day' when burgesses congregated, as since medieval times, to display their weapons for the potential protection of the town. A young boy got hold of a gun, fired it badly, and a piece of burning tow landed on the roof of a house near Rotten Row. As was typical, the roof was thatched with straw, peats or heather. Rotten Row houses were so called from the name 'ratton', meaning undressed timber. Probably the houses in this area were built totally of wood. Fire inevitably spread, ultimately destroying about three-quarters of the town.[113]

The town faced a major rebuilding programme. To assist 'his ain toun' in this, Charles I donated £500 sterling.[114] Some townspeople were wealthy enough to start reparation work immediately; others had to wait for funds from other burghs, to which they had appealed.[115] Much of the wood for rebuilding came from Garvock estate, a mile or so east of the town **figure 1**, where the burgesses had the right to fell. So much was needed that it was said that the policies were denuded. The owner of the estate felt that Garvock mansion house was so spoiled that he moved to his town house in Maygate before transferring to Pitliver, near Charlestown.[116] Although the new dwellings were largely of wood, the solars were usually of stone, which would tend to minimise the risk of further fires. Protocol books give details of many properties at this time. One at the west end of the High Street, for example, consisted of a hall, backstair, forestair, with two rooms above the hall and two 'laich' or low houses – one functioning as a brewhouse and the other as a cellar. The northmost stair had a further two rooms and a stable. The property had an access to the High Street and also at the foot of the tenement to the kirkyard.[117] This was a somewhat extensive property and probably housed more than one family. It is clear that there were subdivisions to many of the original plots. In 1643 and 1644, for example, resignations of quarter parts of tenements are recorded in Collier Row.[118]

Public buildings had also to be replaced. The grammar school, erected as recently as just after the Reformation, was totally ruined. It was rebuilt on the same site **figure 34**, on Queen Anne Street, where the present General Post Office stands. A small building of about 40 feet in length, 25 feet in breadth and 16 feet in height (12.3 by 7.7 by 4.9 metres), it had two storeys. The upper floor was where the classrooms were situated and this floor was approached by an external staircase.[119] The medieval tolbooth probably also suffered in the fire, for it is known that the house next to it, on the south and further away from the source of the fire, owned by one John Anderson was destroyed. It is possible that the tolbooth, being a considerably more robust building with slated roof, needed only repair rather than total rebuild. It seems that the town had rebuilt itself in a matter of years. A description of High Street in 1635 speaks of wooden fronts on the houses, above the first stone storey. Many of these upper storeys projected and overhung the street. Most had outside stairs giving access to the upper floors, some of these stairs almost intruding into the middle of the street. Traffic – wheeled horse-drawn carts – up and down this market street must have been chaotic. Pedestrians, too, must have struggled – there were no pavements and the thoroughfare was only partly causied or paved; the rest would have been mud. Clearly, the work of Michael the 'caswsamaker' (*see* p 24) had deteriorated. Given that there were supposedly 1,850 people in the town and suburbs attending the market, as well as those who came in from the countryside, congestion must have been intense.[120] It is possible that some funding for material improvements came from the kirk – in 1649 the Kirk Session Records note that an account was submitted to them for the building of Legate's Bridge and the bridge at the end of Netherton.[121]

The parish church (nave of the medieval church)

The parish church, the former nave, needed maintenance throughout all of these rebuilding processes. In 1626 the south-west end required repair. At this time, also, the interiors of reformed churches were being altered to suit the new liturgy. One of the most common additions was the erection of 'lofts', or communal seats, where trade incorporations and others might sit together as a symbol of unity. The scholars' and the sailors' lofts, the latter built by the sailors of Limekilns in 1648, were two such.[122] The smiths and other incorporations also set up their own lofts, as of course did the guildry. This continued into the next century.[123] During 1634, and in the next two decades, a number of new seats were then added (interestingly, many for women, who previously had had to stand to the side or rear of the church);[124] and also a magnificent new pulpit that was fixed to the middle north pillar of the church. Built of oak, it had a protruding iron rod that held an ornamental iron cup to house an hour-glass.[125]

There is note again of urgent upgrading needed in 1647 – the roof and bells were liable to fall down, according to the Kirk Session Records.[126] Quite what was effected is unclear as by 1655 horses were required to bring both timber and slates from Limekilns for the repair of the church and the lead on the roof was also to be mended.[127]

Problems seem to have been ongoing. By 1675, the north wall beside the porch was decaying and a new buttress had to be inserted. The date 1675 may still be seen on the buttress. Being in regular use, the parish church was kept in better condition than the old conventual church – the original choir of the medieval church; and in 1672 in high winds the eastern end of the choir and the Lady Chapel collapsed.[128] But conditions were not ideal in the parish church. It seems that in 1643 the church was not lit on winter evenings – the parishioners were required to bring their own candles.[129]

The kirkyard was not always treated with respect. Cloth that had been woven locally was often laid out to be soaked – the open space of the kirkyard offered a handy bleaching area.[130] The kirkyard itself seems by 1660, and for some time previously,[131] to have become very marshy and swampy and in rainy seasons flooded in places. The kirk session decided to visit everyone in the parish encouraging each to make a 'voluntary contribution', the funds to go towards draining the kirkyard by a gutter that would travel under the graves and then pass out of the kirkyard and into the gutter under the minister's house and presumably then into the Tower Burn.[132] There was a tradition that this swampiness was caused by a burn that flowed out of a pool to the east of the Friars' Yard – this would site the pool between the top of the present St Margaret Street and New Row and was probably the erstwhile 'fish pond' of the Benedictine monks. There were no gates to the kirkyard until 1707. In consequence animals – cows, pigs and dogs – entered and trampled the ground, so a wright was given 40 shillings Scots to set up pillars to keep them out.[133]

Keeping order

The town had to deal with other perceived problems. There seem to have been two places where witches and warlocks were 'tried' and punished. After considerable mistreatment and provocation in the tolbooth the supposed culprit might be taken up Townhill Road or to an area near the present Bellyeoman Road. Supposed witches were burnt at the Witch-Loan, near to Bellyeoman Road in 1643;[134] a little to the south was the witches' dub where suspected witches were drowned. This was not filled in until 1791, although it ceased to function as a place of supposed witch persecution a century before[135] and was still noted on maps post-dating 1791. To the north, between Headwell and Townhill **figure 1**, stood the town gallows, thus giving the name 'Gallowgait' to the road leading east from the East Port. Other forms of punishment were the humiliation of standing with the branks, a scold's bridle, in the mouth on market day, when there were plenty of people around to witness the disgrace, being carted and scourged through the town and then branded and banished from

the burgh or being incarcerated in the 'limehouse'. This last seems
to have been a cellar in the tolbooth sometimes used to ward female
delinquents.[136] It gained its name from its other function of being the
storehouse of lime 'shells' which had been burnt at Limekilns but not
yet slaked. It was essential to keep them dry until the slaking process
when they were needed at the lime 'pots' nearby, close to St Catherine's
Chapel. Punishment might also involve being taken from the prison,
placed at the tron – on a market day – with a paper on the forehead
detailing the misdemeanour, but if the misdemeanour was fornication
the woman had her hair clipped as well.[137] Other systems of public
confession of sins might involve being placed at the 'jougs' or being
ducked into water on the cukstool, as in medieval times.[138] The stocks
were still also in use for offenders against the public weal.[139] Little had
changed since the public humiliation displayed in the punishments of
the Middle Ages. Dunfermline was also, along with many other towns,
obviously suffering from 'idle beggars and vagabonds' and orders were
given that a house of correction should be built in 1672.[140]

Battle of Inverkeithing

The Battle of Inverkeithing on 19 July 1651 was a last stand by
the Scottish army in support of Charles II (1649–85). Under the
leadership of the Cromwellian generals, Overton and Lambert, the
remnant of the defeated army was pursued to Dunfermline. The
parish church was broken into, money was stolen and furnishings were
broken. The Cromwellian troops were then billeted in the unwilling
town until the end of September. But greater damage was done by
their presence. It is said that they destroyed St Mary's Chapel in the
Netherton and also St Leonard's Chapel and Almshouse.[141] It would
seem that the latter was certainly cast down. A small house south of
St Leonard's, now gone, had a lintel-stone dated 1666. Tradition
had it that the house was built from the stones of the chapel and
almshouse.[142]

The natural environment

What had changed radically in the townscape and environs from the
time of Malcolm Canmore was that the great forest of Dunfermline
had now almost totally disappeared. A small remnant was said to be
left – at Golfdrum and Buffie's Brae – in 1700[143] and possibly also
in the Woodmill area; but this too would soon disappear. In the late
sixteenth or early seventeenth century, coal working began to increase
in importance for the town, possibly because the countryside had
been largely denuded of trees. Fortunately for the preservation of old
buildings, there are no significant coal seams under the central part

of Dunfermline itself. Although important coal seams such as the Dunfermline Splint are present in a semicircular arc round the west, north and east of the town, they are usually masked by a covering of boulder clay. At Wellwood that is as much as 70 feet (21.5 metres) thick but at Berrylaw and West Baldridge it is only 15 feet (4.6 metres) thick and in Townhill the cover is only three to nine feet (1.9 to 2.8 metres) and more sandy, so it would have been easier to penetrate for early workings.

Despite the clay cover, the early miners would have been able to get an idea of the presence of coal seams from outcrops in the Broomhead Burn and Baldridge Burn **plate 10**.[144] A complaint to the town council by the laird of Middle Baldridge in 1624 that the townspeople were stealing his coal makes it clear that mining was being undertaken in Baldridge.[145] And by 1670 there are references to mining in Townhill.[146] Less important coal workings were also located in Halbeath around this time.[147] It is known that there was limited coal-mining carried out by the monks of Dunfermline Abbey because a charter of 1291 gave them the right to obtain coal in 'the lands of Pittencrieff'.[148] The medieval town burgesses may have had the right to work coal on the town muir, in the Townhill area, but the extraction of peat was probably more important for them. It is interesting, therefore, that as late as 1668 the council was laying down regulations to control the manner in which the town peat was being dug.[149] But, clearly, coal-mining was on the increase, so much so that in 1700 the council appointed one Patrick Angus to be the tacksman of the town coal, giving him authority to hold courts at the coal hill where he might fine colliers, bearers and anyone else involved in the extraction process, reserving to the bailies the right to adjudicate between the tacksman and the colliers if appeal was made to them.[150] The routeway down the west side of Pittencrieff Park, still called the Coal Road, is a reminder of the strong economic importance of the industry.[151]

The end of the seventeenth century

As the seventeenth century closed, there were around 2,000 inhabitants in Dunfermline. This was no longer a small town.[152] The Hearth Tax returns of 1691, instigated for the purposes of taxation, suggest that the vast majority of dwellings were still small, however, some 170 out of 273 properties in the town having only a single hearth, and only 14 properties with five or more hearths.[153] And the 'Register containeing [sic] the State and Condition of Every Burgh Within the Kingdome of Scotland' compiled in 1692 deduced that the town's income was' £1,106 17s., whereas outgoings, even with certain unquantifiable expenses, were £1,154 16s.[154]

The eighteenth century

The economic and physical state of the town

Whatever the town's financial situation at the beginning of the century, Dunfermline considered it dire, with an appeal being made to the Convention of Royal Burghs for financial support.[155] Impressive renovations and innovations were effected, however, in the townscape over the next hundred years.

The town ports

It was reported in 1702 that both the East and Cross Wynd Ports were in such a poor state that they were liable to collapse.[156] Three years elapsed before one James Meldrum was instructed to repair the East Port; it would seem, however, that little or nothing was done, as in 1718 the port seems to have fallen down and orders were given for it to be rebuilt.[157] Its time was limited, however. Both the East and Cross Wynd Ports were removed in 1752,[158] probably because they were proving an encumbrance to traffic and their original medieval function was now defunct. Two years later Collier Row or Mill Port suffered the same fate.[159] By 1765 complaints were being lodged with the town council that the West Port **figure 11** at St Catherine's Wynd was also becoming dangerous. This also was demolished in 1780 – probably the last of the town ports to go.[160]

Road improvements

Spittal Bridge **figure 10a** was a vital access and exit point to and from North Queensferry and Rosyth. It was reported as in a poor state in 1703 and rebuilt three years later.[161] Similarly, the entrance and exit to the town from the west, via the Tower Hill, was of crucial importance. The council ordered in 1710 that funding should be allocated to the 'cutting of the tower hill to make the highway straight'.[162] This probably meant that part of the Tower Hill was cut away to make the access to the town less steep. In 1788 the Tower Bridge, or gyrth bow, was rebuilt **figure 18**.[163] An extant map of 1766 **plate 3** clearly shows the bridge to be already double levelled.[164]

The maintenance of minor roads within the town was also monitored. The Foul Vennel, or In Below the Wa's, was clearly living up to its name – instructions were given in 1734 that it should be cleaned and kept in proper order.[165] Similar problems were occuring in Rotten Row – there was such an accumulation of rubbish that water was gathering in the middle and, when frozen, causing a dangerous passage.[166] Other factors were damaging the town's streets.

By 1752 the town authorities took action against those who were carting coal through the town from Baldridge coal hill to the coast. The weight of their loads was harming the road surfaces, particularly in Collier Row, which according to a 1766 map **plate 3** was narrow at both its south and north ends, but somewhat bulbous in the middle.[167] In future, anyone not taking the official route – Back Row (Queen Anne Street) and New Row would be fined – six pence per load carried on the back and nine pence per cart load.[168] The continual renewal of this bye-law suggests that the carriers took little notice.

The town also made distinct investment in the creation of new roads. In 1752, property was purchased with the aim of carving a new street to lead south from the market cross – initially called New Street, but from 1809 Guildhall Street.[169] This superseded an earlier lane, some seven to eight metres to the east, Christison Hill Lane. This was an old footpath, possibly the post-Reformation link between the upper and lower town over the one-time gardens of the monastery. Some of the buildings on the site of the edge of the lane, such as stables, may still be found behind the shops and offices of Guildhall Street, now serving as offices, restaurant and photographic premises. In 1810 the Foul Vennel was also to be upgraded to the status of a road. On a 1766 map **plate 3** it was already marked as relatively wide, but called 'Monastery Wall'.[170] The council purchased land from the owners of the backlands of the High Street, further widened the vennel and began the construction of a new road – Canmore Street.[171] Saint Margaret Street was also started, also temporarily called the New Street or the New Road and, according to a 1766 map, 'Shore gait', as a continuation of Guildhall Street. To fund all of these innovations the council decided to levy a tax of two pence on a pint of ale.[172]

Probably the most significant of these innovations was the building of Bridge Street. The owner of Pittencrieff, Mr George Chalmers, proposed to the town council in 1765 that a bridge should be built over the Tower Burn in a line with the High Street, the tolbooth would be removed **figure 20** and the old route west by Tower Hill would be abandoned. This was debated often by the council and two years later work began.[173] The work was financed largely by Chalmers and completed in 1770. The roadway over the bridge – usually called the New Bridge – began two years later. Under the keystone of the bridge on the south face of the arch may still be seen the coat of arms of Chalmers. It is very clear that this new route suited the proprietors of Pittencrieff, as their property of Pittencrieff ceased to be the main route to the west. Indeed, by 1771, the women of the town who had been accustomed to use the area to the north side of Tower Hill for washing, drying and bleaching linen were not allowed access, as the property was enclosed and deemed to be private land.[174] There were, however, more than 1,200 living on the estate of Pittencrieff in the

20 Tolbooth demolished to make way for Bridge Street (from D Thomson)

1790s.[175] Many others had already been relocated, being given feus on Bridge Street.[176]

Further north, a less ambitious bridge was constructed in 1766 **plate 3**, as seen on a contemporary map[177] – over Buffie's Brae Burn. Until this time the water was crossed by planks and stepping stones.[178] Three years later, it is interesting to note in the burgh records the purchase by the council of a small close – a mere four feet (1.2 metres) wide – that led from High Street to Rotten Row. This, with further purchases of land and property, would eventually become South Chapel Street in 1804.[179]

The council's investment in new and better thoroughfares continued. Gibb Street was begun in 1771 and ten years later a new road from Gibb Street to Netherton (Moodie Street) began to have houses built on it.[180] This replaced an older road aligned slightly to the west. The following year the Common Vennel was upgraded to Priory Lane; and the Golfdrum fields, where there were only about a dozen huts, were aligned with Buffie's Brae, to ultimately create Golfdrum Street.[181] Further developments resulted from the opening up of the New Bridge (Bridge Street). Chalmers Street, Woodhead Street and Pittencrieff Street began to be laid out. There had been scattered settlement in these vicinities before the building of the bridge, but access had been down back closes from the back of the tolbooth and Collier Row and over the burn, either by planks or stepping stones.[182] It is interesting to note from the burgh records that, in spite of such improvements, Cross Wynd as late as 1793 afforded only six feet (1.8 metres) of space for carts to pass, as a result of the forestairs on either side of the wynd protruding into the street. The council determined in January of that year to enter into negotiations to purchase these forestairs in order to open up the roadway.[183]

A number of Dunfermline's closes still exist. Most of the tenement buildings had closes that gave access (the old 'ische and entrie', (*see* p 28) to backyards, drying greens and rear stairs to upper floors. Examples can be seen in Reid Street, Priory Lane, Hill Street, Campbell Street and elsewhere. Some closes became rights of way, but were few and far between. A map of *c.*1775[184] shows only two such between Queen Anne Street and High Street – Horsemarket Close (Douglas Street when it was widened in1830)[185] and Fleshmarket Close (later South Chapel Street and then by 1828 Randolph Street).[186] To the south of High Street, closes developed, possibly as a result of leaving gaps between buildings as a fire barrier. Free School Close, so named from the Free School that stood on the west side at the top of the close, is shown on John Wood's map of 1823 **figure 4**. Music Hall Lane (once Fish Market Close) to the west of Guildhall Street took its current name from the music hall established in 1852, to the east, capable of holding 1,500 people.[187] Wilson's Close lies a little further west, having had other previous names, such as Ho' Boy's Close and Dairy Close. Blelloch's Close also united High Street and Maygate, a convoluted route which may have combined two separate closes, one leading from Maygate, the other from High Street.[188]

Improved access both east and west was also under way. The route west by the Urquhart Cut began to be formed by blasting with gunpowder in 1775; and to the east the road to Kirkcaldy was aligned to the south of the town green, near Garvock, rather than to the north at the foot of Witch Loan.[189] Inevitably, all of this came at a high cost to the town and in 1790 toll bars were set up[190] at the town green, the Spittal, Limekilns Road, Baldridge Burn and Pittencrieff Street.[191]

Public buildings

As in the Middle Ages, public buildings were a constant drain on the town's finances. One of the rooms in the lower floor of the tolbooth had functioned as a meal market from 1740, the town lacking an alternative venue.[192] In 1751 the tolbooth roof required reslating; the timber was sound, being of oak.[193] Three years later, human intervention caused damage. The north-east corner of the tolbooth and the fence round the nearby Tron Burn (interestingly, presumably no longer flagged) were so affected by coal carts coming down Collier Row that there was fear that they might fall down.[194] The tolbooth, however, was to have a limited life. According to the burgh records, it was demolished in May and June 1769 to make way for Bridge Street (*see* p 41). The fan-shaped steps with the passage-way and

Tolbooth Port underneath **figure 20**, the prisons, the limehouse (*see* p 38) and the council chambers disappeared.[195] Within two years the old tolbooth had been replaced by a new town-house,[196] on a site a little further south, leaving clear the access to Bridge Street. Concern was raised at this point about the cost of covering the steeple with copper; a cheaper option was chosen and the steeple was coated in blue slate. Below ground level there were four rooms – one for the keeper of the town-house, the next functioned as a prison – 'a black hole for desperadoes' – and the other two housed the town's lamps, oil and the scavengers' brooms. The street level contained the council room, the clerk's writing rooms and a closet.[197] It was not long, however, before there were complaints that this accommodation was too small and by 1793 preparations were in hand to add two storeys.[198] These were completed by 1795.

The market cross, although a smaller structure, needed maintenance; and by 1740 was even, according to the records, in danger of falling down.[199] With the opening of Guildhall Street (*see* p 41) it was felt that the cross was an obstruction on the thoroughfare and in 1752 the council took the decision to remove it.[200] The old tron, where the butter market was held, was also removed in 1765, again to make the town more negotiable by the removal of obstructions and also to enlarge the fish market. It was replaced with a weighing crane to the north of the High Street and near to Bruce Street.[201] The pillory, which stood close to the old tron, was also removed in 1775. The 'cleeks' or restraining irons were, however, secured to the east side of the new town-house for further use. The gallows, which stood near Headwell approaching Townhill, were, according to tradition, stolen in 1757 by a weaver who sawed them up to make into a loom.[202]

Town improvements

Congestion in the town centre became worse in 1702 when the council decided to move the cattle market from Netherton to Collier Row and Rotten Row. By 1713 a decision had been taken to move it once again from this central location to the New Row.[203] The records suggest, however, that the medieval practice of slaughtering in the public highways continued. As late as 1773, the town council were instructing that 'killing swine or other bestial on the High Street' would merit a fine of one shilling.[204] In an attempt to control matters the town council purchased an open area called 'Gibb's square yard', a little to the west of the site of the original market cross, in 1786 to function as a flesh market.[205] In association with this, the council proposed to erect a slaughter-house. Objections were raised to its projected siting in Queen Anne Street and it was ultimately decided to place it at the corner of Knabbie Street (later Carnegie Street).[206]

This preoccupation with animals suggests that Dunfermline, in spite of the many extensive townscape improvements, remained in many respects a rural town. In 1702 the town was supporting a horse race from the town green east to Buckie Burn and back, as well as a foot race. But horses also proved a nuisance. In 1755 the council decided that too many of the townspeople were watering their horses at the High Dam. To prevent this misuse of the town's water, the street leading to the rear of the dam was to be uplifted and the stones put to other uses.[207] It was even claimed that in places High Street had grass growing in it and cows and horses grazed there.[208] Improvements were afoot, however. The council made preparations to remove outshot stairs that impeded the thoroughfare in 1772 and in 1787 High Street and part of Bridge Street were given their first pavements.[209]

The lade, sometimes called the Tron Burn, ran down from the dammed loch (the High Dam), which was on the site of the current Thomson's 'World of Furniture'. By 1701, it was routed as an open waterway on the east side of Collier Row and then led into Maygate.[210] The year 1758 proved to be a year of 'fever'. Many died both in the town and surrounding villages. Probably as part of the efforts to sanitise the town it was decided by the council that the Tron Burn should be cleaned out of its accumulated trash, as was Gibb's Well in Fleshmarket Close at 'Gibb's square yard' to the north of High Street, which was polluted with 'nastiness', and was for health reasons to be kept locked in future.[211] Saint Margaret's Well, at the north of Headwell Farm was also cleaned out at council expense.[212] That hygiene standards were still at a low level is clear. The town had a 'scavenger', but in 1750 there were still midden heaps lying in the streets.[213]

In 1792 the town green was planted with fir trees around its extremity. By 1795 upgrading was completed and the green now had a fine walking path and pond.[214] Tree planting had also been taking place earlier – in 1729 – near the Heugh Mills, to the west of the palace and up to Tower Hill **plate 4** and on the floor of the old palace. In 1780, the burgh muir was also planted with trees.[215]

Private property developments were also closely monitored. The Dean of Guild Court Records indicate that care was taken over property boundaries, so avoiding encroachment into a neighbour's land; the 'lights' of a neighbour were to be respected and not blocked; and privacy was protected by refusal to allow windows being opened onto a neighbour's close or property. Tenants had the right to complain if the landlord did not maintain his property. The Cross Chamber above the pend or west entry into the town, for example, was deemed to be so unsafe in 1765 that 'the lieges [were] not in safety to pass at or by the East gavil [gable] thereof within the churchyard, the gavil is much off the plumb and it and the side walls rent from top to bottom in places'. Instructions were given that the Cross Chamber should be taken down or the court would order that this would be done at the expense of the owner. Instructions were also given that, on re-building of property, walls once of stone and mud should now be of a more substantial construction of stone and lime.[216]

The abbey complex

Gradually, throughout this century, the abbey and palace complex became defunct or increasingly the province of the laity. By 1708, the palace had become so neglected that the north wall and part of the roof collapsed.[217] Eight years later, possibly also due to neglect, but also caused by the undermining of the structure by the digging of graves in the old choir, the lantern tower which stood at the junction of the nave and choir of the church collapsed.[218] Worship continued in the parish church, however, with an element of dispute over who had rights to seats, and much discussion as to whether pews should be built, rather than seats, to accommodate more people.[219] Repairs of the parish church, however, were effected in 1728 and again in 1734.[220] In 1734 the inhabitants of Netherton were given permission to access the erstwhile abbey lands by the nether-gate, or lower gate **plate 6**, to the abbey. In the same year, a portion of the abbey wall to the north, between Abbot Street and Canmore Street, was demolished to give access to the new bleachfields in the Abbey Park area (*see* p 48).[221] Four years later, a section of the southerly wall along the Common Vennel (Priory Lane) fell as a result of neglect. That to the north was clearly in a dangerous state, complaints being made in 1743 and in the following year.[222] Much of this was removed in 1762. In 1766 the ruined Lady Chapel was partially removed to provide space for a burial ground for the Elgin family.[223]

It is interesting to note that in 1740 a third storey was added to Pittencrieff House – supposedly with stones from the palace and abbey ruins.[224] There are a number of properties, some still standing, that may have benefited from the decay of the abbey/palace complex **plate 7**. In 1753 the last remnants of the monks' dormitory proved a useful source of stone for a stable and byre on the same site.[225] A final indicator of the old abbey's demise came in 1762 when a new street – known from 1811 as Monastery Street – from the Abbey Close to the top of the Limekilns Road was opened up. The public now had full access across the monastery lands, saving them from the now defunct, but possibly unofficial, route through the Pittencrieff policies along a path at the foot of the palace.[226]

A major change came to church worship in this century. Ralph Erskine, who had been ordained to the second charge in the Dunfermline parish in 1711, and promoted to the first charge in 1716, seceded from the established church in 1736. Dunfermline's first Secession Church, of which he was minister, was opened in Queen Anne Street.[227] The church built for Erskine was demolished and the statue of Erskine marks the location of the pulpit of the original church. The now vacated building – St Andrew's Erskine Church'– was designed by David Whyte in 1798–1800.[228]

Old chapels

Saint Leonard's Chapel **plate 2** was ruinous by the second half of the century. Varying accounts say that in 1756 the south wall and part of the east collapsed; alternatively, they were still upstanding although in poor condition in 1779. By 1798 it seems that the remnants collapsed and the chapel and the associated graveyard ceased to exist.[229]

Saint Mary's Chapel, which stood near the north end of the present Elgin Street across from Moodie Street, suffered a similar fate. It was reportedly in ruins by 1783; and the final traces were removed in 1814.[230] Saint Margaret's Cave or Oratory **figure 21**, however, apparently still housed a stone table and seat as late as 1760.[231]

21 St Margaret's Cave (from E Henderson)

Industry

An innovation for Dunfermline was the introduction of damask weaving in 1718. The secrets of production were supposedly gained by stealth from the damask workers at Drumsheugh, Edinburgh, by James Blake. A skilled weaver, he then set up, with two colleagues, several looms in the Pends, at the southern gatehouse of the royal palace.[232]

A further encroachment into the erstwhile abbey lands came in 1731. The town's linen weavers lacked a decent bleaching field. Representation was made that the Abbey Park would prove a suitable location and within four years canals were being built there under council supervision. The weavers also at this time built a calender house in the New Row **figure 9**.[233] Other New Row occupants, however, caused concern. By 1744, there were fears that the back gates of properties on the west side of New Row – through the old abbey wall – were facilitating illegal access to the bleachfield. All such gates were to be blocked up.[234] The records suggest that the spinners used the north side of Tower Hill (*see* p 41) and St Catherine's Yard for their bleaching.[235] By 1758, however, the town decided to relinquish their agreement on the bleaching green at Abbey Park and the majority of cloth was sent to other towns for bleaching.[236]

The Dean of Guild, David Turnbull, a dyer, set up a dye house nearby in 1752, to the east of the nether mill, [237] in front of the Frater House **figure 27**. Another dyer, William Dickie, came up with a greater innovation in 1783. He set up an indigo mill – the first in Dunfermline – which was activated by a large dog, which ran round a wheel as a treadmill.[238]

It is interesting to note in the Guild Merchant Records that the authorities made efforts not only to provide charity, but also to encourage employment skills. In 1718, £3 was given to Isobel Wilson, probably the widow of a guild brother, but she received further charity – £7 'to help her pay her son's prentice fee'.[239]

Production of textiles was such that the town council decided to establish a market specifically for yarn and cloth in 1753. This was held beside the tron every Friday between the hours of nine and eleven in the morning; and, to encourage outsiders to patronise the market with their home-spun goods, accommodation was set aside to keep any unsold goods until the following market.[240] Bishop Richard Pococke, touring Scotland in 1760, arrived in Dunfermline and commented on the thriving town – making 'much table linnen [*sic*] of all kinds, ticking, carpets, and striped woolen stuffs for women ware'.[241] By 1792, there were 1,200 looms in the town[242] and a flax mill at Brucefield, claiming to be the second, but probably the third, in Scotland with the patent for spinning sourced by water power, employed 150.[243] A visitor in 1799 rated Dunfermline a 'considerable manufacturing town'.[244]

The Heugh Mills **plate 5** feature often in the contemporary records. In 1732, the corporation of bakers was given the right to build a mill and use water to run it and also to winnow and dry the wheat in Abbey Close. It seems that wind power was also used as the following year a complaint was put to the council by the tenant at the Heugh Mills that 'want of wind', as a result of the tree planting nearby, restricted the winnowing process (*see* p 56). The council agreed to contribute £24 to assist in the erection of 'fanners' for the winnowing process.[245] By 1739, machinery had been placed in the building below the corn mill for the grinding of snuff – apparently the first snuff mill in the town.[246] The Collier Row mill still functioned but was in need of repair – it needed re-slating in 1739 and the town deemed that this should be effected at the tenant's expense.[247] It seems, however, that the mills were not proving too profitable by 1755. The tenant of the Collier Row Mill and the Heugh Mills had agreed to move out, but had arrears of rent. When asked by the town council what funds he had to settle these, he confirmed that he had only two cows, seven pigs, household goods and work tools. The livestock was put up for sale and the council attempted to let the mills by roup – but there were no bidders.[248]

Although the town received rentals from the mills, their upkeep seems to have been a drain on the town's finances and in 1768 the Collier Row Mill and Heugh Mills, along with some abbey lands were sold firstly to Mr Black, former clerk of the Regality of Dunfermline, some time between 1758 and 1760[249] and then to Mr Chalmers of Pittencrieff. In addition, another flour mill was built at the Heugh Mills site in 1784–5, using water power. It was converted to steam in 1819.[250] Thomas Pennant on visiting the town in the 1770s noted:

> the town wants the advantage of a river, but has a small stream for economic uses, which is conducted through the streets in a flagged channel. At its discharge, it joins another rivulet, then arriving at a fall into a wooded dell of a hundred feet in depth, becomes then again useful in turning five mills, placed one below the other, with room for as many more.[251]

His mention of 'another rivulet' is probably a reference to the outfall from the abbey which joined the lade around the area of the current War Memorial **figure 34**. The five mills spoken of may have included the Collier Row and Lady's Mill, as well as the Heugh Mills.

Other industries could be seen around the town. In 1740 two roods of land to the east of the Heugh Mills were leased to a shoemaker to set up a tanning works.[252] A further tan works was set up at Clayacres in 1799. By 1777 a spade manufactory had also been established beside the lower Heugh Mills. At a little distance, at the east end of Bee Alley Gardens (St Margaret Street), a distillery was opened in 1782. And it is said that in 1788 there were seven breweries producing 'Dumfarlin nut-broon ale'.[253]

Mining was of growing importance to the town. Workings in Baldridge, Townhill and Halbeath further developed, though these mines were probably relatively small scale in the eighteenth century, with whole families helping get the coal to the surface. From around the middle of this century, and certainly by 1800, Pittencrieff Colliery, based around 'Coaltown (Pittencrieff)' as marked on Wood's plan of 1823 **figure 4**, was an important site. It was not until 1775 that the town's colliers were emancipated, becoming freed men, as opposed to serfs tied to a particular location.[254]

Further townscape changes

Water supply was an essential provision in the town. The council attempted to provide adequate access to water. The stairs that led up to the High Mill Dam were to be repaired as well as those down into the dam in 1760 so that people could bucket out water more easily.[255] The Head Well, once called St Margaret's Well, as one of the principal sources of water, was inspected and upgraded regularly.[256] By 1763 the council was considering a supply brought in pipes from the Town Loch **figure 1** but this was rejected and by the following year instruction was given to start the laying of pipes from the Head Well.[257] This 'St Margaret's Well Water Scheme' was completed in 1765, although modifications continued until 1778, the supply terminating in a cistern at the current Douglas Street. The supply was not adequate for the whole town and in the same year six public wells were to be provided – at the Tron, the foot of Rotten Row, Maygate, at the Horse Market at the foot of Reservoir Close, the top of the New Row in East Port Street and in the new Guildhall Street.[258] In 1773, the townspeople were objecting that one of their customary sources of water – the 'Well of Spaw' or 'Wallace Spa' – some 50 yards south of Tower Hill, was having its access blocked by Mr Chalmers, proprietor of Pittencrieff.[259]

Fire had been a constant hazard with wooden buildings so liable to combustion. In spite of the fact that, increasingly, stone and slates were used instead of wood and thatch, there remained a danger. In 1721 the council authorised the purchase of hide from Edinburgh to make fire buckets. By 1760, when the fire buckets were being inspected, although in good order, they numbered only 18. It is not surprising that the townspeople deemed that a 'fire machine' would be an asset to the town in 1785 and the council offered ten guineas towards its purchase.[260] If it was bought it was of little effect by 1809 when the Rotten Row burned down (*see* p 53).

It is interesting to note that the burgh's marches were still upheld as important in this century, as they had been in the previous.[261] In 1704, the council decreed that everyone on entering as a burgess should finance the erection of a new march stone. Six years later, all the burgesses were summoned to meet on horseback or on foot to ride the marches. Those who failed to meet at 'Craigncat' and could not answer to the roll-call were to be fined.[262] (The Craigencat Crags were south-east of Loch Glow near Craigencrow, on the border between the old Dunfermline and Cleish parishes.) The riding of the marches continued until at least 1756.[263]

The town had a number of schools, as well as the official grammar school. Some were not registered. One Francis Paterson, for example, held a school for boys and girls in 1727 in the room above the gateway of Queen Anne's house, adjacent to the west side of the steeple. It was still in existence in 1742. A sewing school was set up in Cross Wynd around 1764, apparently attracting some 30 to 40 pupils, some travelling from Lochgelly. Three years later, one John Reid opened up a school in the Horse Market at the east end of High Street before moving to Rotten Row. As well as the usual academic subjects he also instructed in navigation, land surveying and the use of globes; he was so popular that pupils travelled to the school from far and wide.[264]

Street lighting was a further innovation. Six lamps were purchased in 1752. The council was so impressed with them that a further six were ordered. Two years later, three more were bought.[265] The town now had the benefit of 15 oil lights at night.

The homes of the people were improving throughout the century. The Window Tax, first levied in 1748, gives an insight into the number of windows in Dunfermline homes, so indicating the size of the properties. There were some clearly substantial dwellings in the town, with 11–24 windows. The most prominent stood just outside the burgh **figure 1** – Hill House boasted 68, Pitfirrane and Pitreavie both with 66, Pittencrieff with 61, and Broomhall with 36 in 1748.[266]

The new roadways and streets meant a significant change in the townscape. The cannibalisation of the abbey precincts also brought a differing living pattern. The pends were occupied largely by tradesmen, paying rental to Chalmers, the owner of Pittencrieff.[267] Anne of Denmark's house and the two constabulary houses, having had the indignity of being occupied by Jacobite forces in the 'Fifteen' rising, had become so ruinous by 1797 that they were sold and demolished.[268]

The nineteenth century

Population

Some indication of the increase in population over the previous century may be gauged by the fact that, compared with the one parish church in 1700, there were by 1800 ten churches and meeting houses. The town had 14 schools, 26 linen manufacturers, about 800 weavers, 88 wrights, 57 smiths, 51 shoemakers, 41 masons, 20 bakers, 47 tailors and nine fleshers. The population in the town and its immediate suburbs was 5,484, inhabiting in the town itself 705 houses.[269]

New streets

With extensive improvements to the street system in the last century, even more was effected in the nineteenth century. The council subscribed ten guineas towards a public subscription to purchase a piece of land to widen Maygate in 1802.[270] The following year, two closes were conjoined, with old properties being demolished, to form South Chapel Street (later Randolph Street). The weather was such, however, that in the autumn of that year all the streets were flooded and the Baldridge Burn Bridge was swept away.[271] The year 1820 saw the feuing of Reid's Park and the beginning of the construction of Reid Street, largely replacing the old pathway called Gilley's or Gillie's Wynd. At the foot of this wynd the pathway had once continued opposite the end of Reid Street as Sand Road, meeting the Rosyth Road near to the Grange Farm. It is reputed to have received the name from the sand carried up it to repair work in the abbey.[272] Inglis Street was laid out, with the first houses being built in 1821. Removal of old property and back dykes to the medieval tofts opened up the way for Douglas Street in 1830.[273] The town council was clearly innovative – £10 was allocated towards experiments to assess the viability of a tunnel under the Forth in 1807[274] – not achieved even two hundred years later!

Civic improvements

Other civic improvements were effected, some of which may still be recognised today. In 1807 on the site of two 'worthless old tenements' on the south side of the Cross, the 'Cross Buildings' or guildhall was founded. Work was completed by the following year, apart from the steeple – not finished until 1811 – and some interior flooring which was in place by about 1817 when it became the Spire Inn and Hotel. Still standing today, it is now an empty restaurant

complex and has previously served as the sheriff court and a
government job centre.[275]

Public baths were apparently erected in Queen Anne Street in
1844; but on 12 July 1877 the vastly improved baths donated by
Andrew Carnegie were opened by him in School End Street.[276]
They were replaced in 1903 by a new bath and gymnasium complex,
again paid for by Andrew Carnegie, on the east side of Pilmuir
Street. Still standing, with renovations and extensions, but largely in
original state, the magnificent Carnegie Baths are a well-loved site in
the town. Other amenities were available to the townspeople, such as
the Music Hall. Capable of holding 1,500 people, its main entrance
was from Guildhall Street and it opened with a grand concert on 30
December 1852.[277]

Another feature on the present townscape is the City Hotel. Built
around the turn of the eighteenth and nineteenth centuries, it retains
much of the early façade and has been known by various names,
such as New Inn, McLean's Inn and, from the 1870s, The City Arms
Hotel. A topographical feature was the Dunfermline Co-operative
Society store which has disappeared only recently, built originally
at the top of Randolph Street. The foundation stone was laid in
1866. The site, which has been derelict for a few years, has clear
archaeological potential because of its situation in the heart of
medieval and post-medieval Dunfermline.

The year 1876 was to see a major change on the townscape. The
old town-house was demolished and work began on the present one –
the City Chambers **figure 15**. Also demolished were five houses on
the west side of Kirkgate. One in particular, with a pended gate
to Kirkgate, in the middle of the five, seems to have been of some
quality and had long been known as 'the Danish ambassador's
house', although the ambassadors' houses were possibly sited in
St Catherine's Wynd. The City Chambers were the design of the
Edinburgh architect James Campbell Walker in a combination of
French and Gothic styles. Not including the costs of demolition,
the new municipal building and its site cost over £18,000.[278]

Wooden housing and fire

It is clear, however, that many buildings were of old design – several
still of wood and proving a fire hazard. The year 1809 saw a huge fire
in Rotten Row. The only way to put the fires out was with buckets and
pitchers of water from the dam and the Tron Burn, so presumably the
fire machine was never bought or was by now defunct (*see* p 51). The
following year the council purchased two fire engines, with a full
'complement of fire buckets'. Partially timber buildings survived on
the High Street. One such, of both stone and timber had its frontage

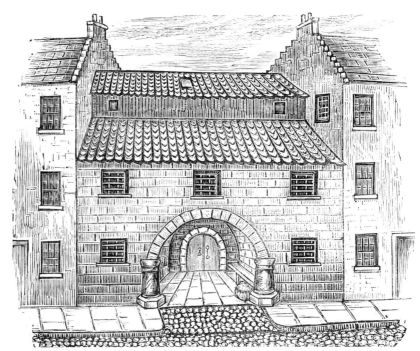

22 left Archway within old Sanctuary House (courtesy of Bert McEwan)

23 right Sanctuary House (from E Henderson)

rebuilt of stone as late as 1825.[279] Other partially wooden buildings survived in the town. One of the very few remaining at the time of writing this Survey was in a poor state on the east side of Bruce Street. Once a jewellers and antique shop, the stone building had a wooden extension that once functioned as a joiner's workshop. This has now been demolished. It was well worthy of an archaeological survey as redevelopment of the area is intended.

Even impressive houses with stone ground floors and elegant arcades often had upper storeys of wood. It is said that the sanctuary house on the north side of Maygate, formerly belonging to the abbey and originally intended for the safe harbouring of debtors and other accused, was largely demolished in 1819, although it may have been rebuilt by a baker of the name of Meldrum in 1816. From contemporary illustrations this would appear to have had a top storey of wood and a 'large vaulted entrance'. Part of the latter has survived and can still be seen at the time of writing **figures 22** and **23**.[280] In other parts of the town, behind modern façades, stone arcading on ground floors is evidence of some rather fine houses **figures 24** and **25**, although these, too, probably had wooden upper storeys.

24 Demolished house
with arcading
in Douglas Street
(from P Chalmers)

25 Evidence of arcading
at 32 Maygate
(courtesy of
Bert McEwan)

Further improvements

A Municipal Improvement Act of 1811 set the marker for further improvements to the townscape. The act included many matters from pavements to street lighting, demolition and correct build of new houses, water supply, sewage and countless other material matters. At this point the burgh boundaries were also redefined. Many areas of the extended town were now included, except, significantly, the vast majority of Pittencrieff Estate.[281]

Some advances in the water supply had already been effected. From 1805 the public had been allowed under certain conditions to have private water supplies piped to their homes. Not many would have been able to afford this luxury. The following year, the old lead pipes were replaced with new cast-iron ones to bring water via the Head Well to the town's reservoir. Three years later, the council gave financial assistance to the repairing and cleaning of the well, known in medieval times as St Lawrence's Well, and the conduit at Moodie Street.[282] Repairs also seem to have been effected at the watercourse called the Goat. It is still partially visible, to the west of the municipal car park on the site of where it once functioned as an overflow from the Mill Dam down to the Tower Burn. The site of the Mill Dam is now occupied by Thomson's 'World of Furniture', formerly the Canmore Works of J & T Alexander and later Winterthur's silk factory. The Mill Dam itself was possibly filled in when the Canmore Works were erected in 1867.[283] The Little Dam stood nearby, on the corner of Knabbie Street (now Carnegie Drive) and Damside Street (now the extension of Bruce Street). This was filled in in 1886 and a warehouse, part of the Caledonia Works, was erected over it.[284]

It seems that the old lade still ran down its old route – past Headwell Farm, where there was a lock-keeper's cottage, past Grant's Bank (Pilmuir Street) and down Foundry Street, where an inverted syphon had to be inserted to allow the smooth passage of water to the Mill Dam at the point where the new railway system intersected with the lade. By this time, the lade followed a slightly altered route to that of medieval times. It passed down the east side of Bruce Street, moving eastwards along the north side of Maygate, turning southwards down the current St Margaret's Street, along a line under the present Carnegie Library through the abbey lands to Monastery Street, where it proceeded to power the Heugh Mills.[285] It may have been this conduit that was discovered in the abbey lands in 1859.[286]

In 1846 a new water company was formed with share capital subscribed of £13,500. This was occasioned not only by the increasing population, but also the expanding industries in the town (*see* pp 60–63). The water was to be brought from reservoirs built at Craigluscar and was completed by 1850.[287] By 1875, however, there were demands for an even greater supply. The River Devon was considered a potential source, but the Glensherup Burn, a tributary of the Devon, was chosen and the new system was in place three years later.[288] By May 1876, another vital improvement was begun – works for conveying Dunfermline's sewage to Charlestown. This was completed the following year at a cost of about £10,000.[289]

Other upgrading works were seen around the town in this century. In July 1807 the council ordered 34 new lamps – so bringing the street lighting to 106 in the town.[290] Nine more had been added by 1813. The Dunfermline Gas Company was also established in the town in 1828; it soon had set up works at Priory Lane.[291] In 1854 the council ordered that all pavements were to be of stone,[292] rather than dirt or cinders as was normally the case. New slaughterhouses were opened up in Baldridgeburn in 1869.[293] And a wonderful innovation came to the town the following year – a new patent machine for sweeping the streets.

The old abbey and palace complexes

Much of the old stonework was showing signs of the times. In 1807, the south-west tower of the abbey nave, apparently having been dangerous for some time, fell in a thunderstorm as can be seen on **figure 26**. It was replaced some time around 1810 to 1811 with the one that is now extant. Importantly, the foundations of the new Abbey Church, on the site of the old choir, were laid on 10 March 1818. This would become, on completion in 1821, the place of

26 Dunfermline from Bridge Street (from S Hooper)

worship, rather than the old abbey nave, which was not emptied of all seats and church fittings until 1823. Consideration was given to renovation of the old nave in 1820. Instead, the decision was taken to leave it in its essentially medieval state, much as we see it now.[294] In 1824, the final vestige of the old abbey choir – a wall, some 24 feet (7.4 metres) in height, with four gothic windows to the south of the old churchyard, was removed to make way for the northern transept of the new church. Much clearing of the south kirkyard was required after the masons and joiners departed and there was also undertaken at this time levelling of this area that had once been the monastic precincts. Work was also effected in the old – north – kirkyard. It was also levelled, some gravestones being removed and others laid flat. The church environs, however, were not yet salubrious. In 1853, a public subscription raised sufficient money to remove the rubbish and stone between the west door to the church and the Pends. The clutter south of the Pends below the old frater remained. Alarmingly, in 1856 on the south side of the Frater Hall a hole of nine feet (2.8 metres) deep opened up.[295] Now cleared, the refectory and palace ruins are Scheduled Ancient Monuments and properties in the care of Scottish Ministers.

It has been claimed that the palace ruins were 'thoroughly overhauled and repaired' in 1812 by the new proprietor of Pittencrieff, James Hunt. Interestingly for the town, however, after much litigation, in 1871 the House of Lords decided that the palace ruins, and as much land round them as to give access, belonged to the crown and not to James Hunt. While the plea was running Hunt removed the porteress from her cottage. It was said to be sited in a small corner near the square house opposite the abbey, and very picturesque, with its little courtyard walls made of slate and other stones taken from the abbey ruins.[296] The coarsely built wall erected at the end of the previous century to prevent access to the palace by the public was removed four years later. A small wall, with iron rail above, replaced this, giving a full view of the palace.[297]

Schools

Schooling became more customary during the nineteenth century. A number of new schools were founded, some of which retain strong connections with their originals, even if only by name, to this day. The grammar school erected after the fire in 1625 had proved inconvenient and too small (*see* p 35). A new grammar, or high, school was built in 1816–17 in Queen Anne Street on the north side. While the building process was ongoing the pupils occupied the west room of the lower flat of the town-house. Commercial School was also established in 1816. Rolland Street, or Priory Lane, School,

27 Industrial encroachment near the Frater Hall (from W Thomson)

attended by the young Andrew Carnegie, received a bequest of the interest on £1,000 for children whose parents could not afford to pay fees from Mr Adam Rolland of Gask who died in 1763.[298] McLean School followed at Golfdrum in 1842, later moving to Baldridgeburn. Free Churches felt the need to have their own schools and the Free Abbey School opened in 1847–8 in Canmore Street. White tiles behind the Canmore Street Congregational Church are still a reminder of this school.[299] Wilson's School opened in the New Row in 1858; it offered free education to the children of Dunfermline and its suburbs, but a preference was given to those with the surname of Wilson and with parents who were members of the Free Abbey Church. Schools were established also at St Leonard's factory in 1860 – for workers' children (the older ones working half-time in the factory), with a library and reading society[300] – a school name that survives today. And in 1876, Pittencrieff and Milesmark Schools were built. By 1855, the town could even boast of the Dunfermline School of Science and Arts, known also as the School of Design, in the New Row.[301] This became part of the Lauder Technical College established in Priory Lane. Next door in Priory Lane saw the opening, in 1886, of the new grammar school,[302] now converted into flats.

Churches

A number of new churches, accommodating several denominations, was established. The year 1823 saw the formation of a congregation of Roman Catholics, although St Margaret's R C Church in East Port was not opened until 1896. In 1825, the foundation was laid of St Margaret's Presbyterian Church in East Port which was ready for worship the following year. In 1832, the old chapel of ease at North Chapel Street, being considered too small, was demolished and St Andrew's Church was opened for Presbyterian worship the following year. An Episcopal church, the Trinity Episcopal Church – a name transferred to the current building in East Port— was opened in 1842 in Queen Anne Street. Gillespie Church, a well-known feature in Dunfermline to this day, was started in 1848.[303] Several others, for example, were built after this: St John's Parish Church was erected in 1849–50 to a design of the architect Robert Hay, initially as the North Free Church, later to become the United Free, purchased after 1958 as a furniture and retail outlet, now a bar and night club. The old anti-burgher church in Chalmers Street, first built in 1843–4, was removed in 1861 and replaced the following year.[304] The foundation stone of the Free Abbey Church in Canmore Street (later St Paul's – now burned down and a potential site for archaeological excavation) was laid in 1882. This and the Baptist Church in Viewfield Place (East Port) were opened in 1884.

Banking

The proliferation of banks in the town suggests a relatively flourishing economy. Having possibly first been opened on the west side of Bruce Street, at what became known as Kinnis Court **plate 8**, The Bank of Scotland was sited at the west end of Bridge Street in 1801, but had moved to Abbey Park House in 1821, its premises in Bridge Street proving too small.[305] In 1804, a branch of the British Linen Company's Bank was established, as was a branch of the Commercial Bank of Scotland in 1812. The British Linen Bank stood at the foot of Douglas Street.[306] The Dunfermline Savings' Bank, established in 1815, merged with the National Security Savings' Bank in 1838.[307]

Industries and craftsmen

Much of the town's employment was owed to the linen-weaving industry.[308] There were, for example, in 1814, 873 weavers compared to 111 wrights, 68 shoemakers, 52 tailors and 11 fleshers.[309] Table-linen manufactured in Dunfermline, it was thought, brought in £103,020 in the period June 1815 to June 1816;[310] and it was estimated in 1819 that there were 1,507 looms in the parish, with a further 142 in outlying areas such as Carnock, Cairneyhill and Torryburn. These 1,649 looms which looked to the Dunfermline market brought in an estimated annual £120,000.[311] By 1822, it was estimated that there were 1,800 looms in Dunfermline alone. This increased to 2,670 in Dunfermline, with a further 450 in the rest of the parish by 1831.[312] By 1836, goods woven in the town and exported

28 Loom shop floor
(courtesy of papers
of Andy Lawrence)

to America were valued at £153,000, while the home market brought
in £198,700.[313]

The 1840s were, however, a painful period of transition from
hand-loom weaving, often based in private homes, to the factory
system **figure 28**. From the late 1830s, power-loom factories in other
towns, largely manufacturing plain goods, depressed both prices and
wages. Many hand-loom weavers in Dunfermline became destitute
as a result. The year 1842 saw such a level of rioting and looting of
shops by weavers that soldiers were brought in from Edinburgh to
restore order.[314]

By the 1850s, there was an upturn in trade with six firms or
individuals from Dunfermline displaying their work at the Great
Exhibition at Crystal Palace in London. The Pilmuir Works had
already been opened in 1849 and was the first of 11 large steam-
powered damask weaving mills in the town **figure 10b**. In 1851 Messrs
Erskine Beveridge & Co. opened the steam-powered weaving factory
at the site of the old St Leonards Chapel, later employing over 1,000
operatives; the office and warehouse are now flatted **figure 10a**.[315] The
Bothwell Works were established by 1865, followed two years later by
another steam-powered weaving factory at Damside Street – near
the site of the old dam. Named the Canmore Works, it employed
about 850. A further steam-powered factory opened in 1868 – the
Castleblair Weaving Factory – which employed more than 400.[316]
In 1870 St Margaret's Works was opened at Foundry Street by Messrs
Hay & Robertson, with 224 power looms; this expanded rapidly,
having 400 looms by 1882 **figure 10b**.[317]

By 1880 there were 4,000 power looms in Dunfermline, employing 5,000 people; by 1894 this had risen to 5,000 looms and nearly 7,000 employed. The turnover was more than £1million. No wonder that *Campbell's Almanac* of 1875 reported that 'Amid the numerous tall stacks, belching forth their clouds of smoke, the clanking of engines, and the noise of the power loom, were an emigrant to return who had been absent only a few years ... he would not know his own town'.[318]

Spinning on the other hand was in decline. The Dunfermline damask industry had no use for coarse Scottish yarn, needing instead the highest-quality yarn grown in Flanders and spun in Northern Ireland. By 1814 the Brucefield Spinning Mill employed 179 people but closed in 1828, becoming a yarn bleachworks until around 1845. Short-lived was the flax spinning mill, set up in 1814, on the corner of Viewfield Place and East Queen Anne Street. By 1836 there was a peak of seven spinning mills in operation – at Harrie Brae, Golfdrum, Millport at the top of Bruce Street, Knabbie Street, Clay Acres, Milton Green and Midmill; 160 men and the same number of women were employed.[319] These mills fell to five in 1844 and to one in 1864.[320] There were four dye works by the middle of the century.[321] And the weavers had a calender house near to other property they owned in the New Row **figure 9**.[322] The Elgin Bleachfield was opened in 1851. By 1877 it was employing about 50.[323]

Although mainly a textile town, Dunfermline did have other industries. A brick works was established in Woodhead Street (later Chalmers Street) – in 1804. Brick was used in the gables and rear walls of some nineteenth-century buildings, the frontages being of stone, which was more expensive; other properties, for a similar reason, use whinstone in foundations and sandstone gables and rears. A foundry had been sited in Maygate. In 1816 the business was removed to Clayacres. Further iron foundries were also established in and around the town. About two miles north-east of Dunfermline, at Lilliehill, a fire-clay and terracotta works was established in 1867. This works employed about 100 people and the products, such as sewerage pipes and fire bricks, were exported to Scandinavia and the Black Sea.[324] Added to these were three breweries, two tanneries and three ropeworks by the middle of the century.[325]

Coal remained an important economic feature throughout the area. Some of the pits in the area north of Baldridgeburn were in operation until around 1880, when they were recorded as largely exhausted.[326] Pits in Wellwood Colliery, to the north of Dunfermline, were active through the nineteenth century and continued in use into the mid twentieth century. For the burgh, the Townhill coalfield was probably the most important as it was under the control of the burgesses and was worked by the townspeople until around 1838. For financial reasons they leased the field of some 700 acres to a colliery

company around 1840.[327] By 1880 the burgh was receiving lordships,
akin to annual royalties, of over £7,000 per year.[328]

Coal needed to be transported, the most convenient way being
by rail. In 1812, for example, a wagon-way was constructed between
Syme's colliery at Venturefair, one mile north of the town, and the
north of Knabbie Street where the coal depot was sited. In the same
year, the Earl of Elgin had completed a wagon-way from the foot of
the town to his limeworks at Charlestown. This was used also to
convey coal for shipment from Charlestown harbour. The railroad
or wagon-road connecting the Townhill Colliery and the port of
Inverkeithing was completed in 1841.[329] In the nineteenth century
the Town Loch or Moncur was augmented by water pumped
from the coal pits at Townhill, but by 1893 this supply was no
longer available.[330]

Two features of the medieval commercial past were relocated
in the nineteenth century. The weigh beam or weighing crane which
stood at the lower end of High Street was proving an impediment to
pedestrians – the top beam overhung the pavement and the weighing
scales suspended from it swung in the way of those passing by. It was
moved to a close – Black's Close – further up the High Street. The
old market cross had been moved in 1752, its shaft being built into
the corner of a house on the west side of Guildhall Street and its
site marked with stones in the ground. It was re-erected in 1868 by
public subscription; it stood at the corner of Maygate/Kirkgate in the
twentieth century; and it was replaced more or less in its original
position at the foot of Cross Wynd when the High Street was
pedestrianised in the late twentieth century.[331]

Housing

All these industries meant that homes for the people had to be found.
Whereas there had been 6,492 people in the town and its suburbs
in 1811, by 1871 the town had 14,958 inhabitants.[332] The town
expanded, in consequence, with old roads being developed and
new roads being inserted, for example, east of New Row. These
were villas, probably designed to house the wealthier elements of
society, such as linen manufacturers. To ensure that due decorum
was maintained, it was specified that these properties were not to
have pigs in the gardens.[333] Comely Park House was rebuilt in 1785
after being destroyed by fire. Abbey Park House, on Abbey Park
Place, is an outstanding building on the erstwhile abbey lands.
These contrasted sharply with the small weaving houses, often
originally built to house the hand loom on the ground floor, with
living accommodation above. The birthplace of Andrew Carnegie
in 1835, no 2 Moodie Street, is a humble eighteenth-century cottage

and typical. Most houses were single-storeyed with red tiled roofs rather than slate, although those on the outskirts were often thatched.[334] Forestairs were also still to be seen, although the town council had in the 1830s started a policy of removal of forestairs and projecting buildings. It was also decided in 1834 that all houses should be numbered.[335]

All towns had their poor. To accommodate some of them, Dunfermline built a poor house at the old town green in 1843, which could house 130 people. A further sign of poverty was that in this same year the town had no less than 12 pawnbrokers.[336] It was this poorer group of society that suffered most in the cholera epidemic of 1849[337] – first hitting in 1832 and by some blamed on the filthiness of the Mill Dam.[338] The *Dunfermline News* in 1849 reported that from January 1847 to June 1849 some 60 per cent of the entire population of Back Row and the upper part of Bruce Street were affected with typhus fever as a result of the foulness of the dam and mill lade. Requests for their removal or reconstruction were dismissed by Hunt of Pittencrieff and his advisers as 'incompetent'. He was the owner of the site of the dam, half of the town loch and water in the lade;[339] and claimed fees for the use of the water in the lade,[340] Ill-will continued until 1895, Hunt successfully contending that the five manufacturers using the supply should continue to pay up even though the water in the lade was 'a mere driblet'.[341]

Travel

Travel changed vastly in the nineteenth century. A stagecoach called *Antiquary* started to run between Dunfermline and Edinburgh every day apart from Sundays in 1824. Fares were six shillings if seated inside and four shillings if outside. This form of transport ended in 1878. By 1826 a stagecoach from Edinburgh to Crieff called at Dunfermline. The *Aurora* began running between Kirkcaldy and Glasgow in the same year and also stopped in Dunfermline.[342]

There was to be a totally new innovation on Dunfermline's townscape – the arrival of the railway. Early in 1834 a railroad was constructed, joining up the Elgin wagon-road with the lower part of the town, south-west of Netherton. It was used for both goods and passengers from Dunfermline to Charlestown and was pulled by horses. It was claimed that in one year from May 1838 to 1839 almost 23,000 people landed at Charlestown. Most then proceeded north by this railway. A locomotive engine was added to this passenger service in the mid nineteenth century. Not being pulled by horse, the journey could be completed in about ten minutes.[343] Traces of both the wagon-way and the railway may still be detected. Dunfermline's lack of an immediate sea access had been commented

upon a hundred years earlier. It had been mooted that a canal
from Netherton to Charlestown, with a few locks, would have solved
Dunfermline's landlocked situation.[344] This was never taken to
fruition, probably because of the lack of the large volume of water
needed to service locks on canals.

More extensive were the works required to set out the Stirling
to Dunfermline railway. By 1849, spanning the Glen was under
way in the Buffie's Brae area. Five arches were proposed, two
already completed. These are still extant but unused **figure 10b**.
This line would eventually call at what became called Dunfermline's
'Upper Station'. Housing had to be removed to make way for
smaller bridges.[345]

The Edinburgh, Perth and Dundee railway, via Thornton to
Burntisland, was also functioning by 1850, a 'pleasure party group'
arriving to visit the attractions of Dunfermline. The official opening
of the more direct Dunfermline to Edinburgh railway with its station
at Comely Park came in 1877.[346] The arches over the Netherton to
convey the railway are an impressive feature to this day **figure 10a**.
This line terminated at North Queensferry, at which point travellers
were transferred by ferry boat to Port Edgar before continuing
to Edinburgh.

Postscript

There were to be radical changes in the townscape in the twentieth
century.[347] One of the most important for Dunfermline was the
purchase of Pittencrieff estate by Andrew Carnegie in 1902 for the
townspeople. On 30 November 1903, by disposition, the Pittencrieff
policies were transferred to the newly formed Carnegie Dunfermline
Trust for the safekeeping of Pittencrieff on behalf of the people
of Dunfermline.

The following year, sweeping improvements to the townscape
were proposed to the Carnegie Dunfermline Trust by Sir Patrick
Geddes. He considered his report to be 'a plan and plea for
conserving and developing the amenities of a small provincial city,
and its constructive proposals [were] based upon a photographic
survey of its present, and a re-reading of the past'.[348] The proposals
covered many aspects of the historic city. They ranged from
improvements to the railway viaduct **figure 10a** by planting and
landscaping, the upgrading of St Margaret's Cave, the palace
gardens and the environs of the abbey, to the provision of zoos,
aviaries and a 'Hall of Medieval History' in Pittencrieff Park.[349]
He was highly impressed with the 'boulevard' of Comely Park Place
and recommended further planting of trees throughout the town.[350]
In the event, the Carnegie Dunfermline Trust did not take up these

proposals, but the town council did later adopt a policy of tree planting along certain streets. Remnants of these may still be seen at the foot of Maitland Street and top of Elgin Street.

New roads were inserted throughout the century, but perhaps the most contentious came towards the end of this time when a new vehicular route was forced through the public park in 1973–4. Initially opened in 1863 following a gift to the townspeople as a bequest and laid out by Sir Joseph Paxton, there were plans for it to be further extended in 1913. With a new roundabout and entrances to the town, by the 1970s New Row, now truncated,was no longer the important exit road south.

Before the First World War there were more than ten linen factories operating 6,500 looms and employing 7,000, with many more in allied industries such as bleaching, dyeing and transport. Throughout the century all declined and this mainstay of the town by the end of the twentieth century had in effect disappeared.

Expansion of the town was inevitable. The development of housing to the south to Pitcorthie was overshadowed by the vast eastern expansion scheme undertaken at the end of the century. Still ongoing, a vast new Dunfermline is being created. Out-of-town superstores have had an impact on the now pedestrianised High Street. But plans are afoot in the twenty-first century to regenerate the old historic centre. It is hoped that this will be effected with sympathy for Dunfermline's historic past. Much has already been lost but there is much still to conserve.

Notes

1 *Chron. Fordun*, liber v, 213.
2 *Dunf. Reg.*, nos 1 and 2.
3 Taylor, 'Welcome to Fothrif'.
4 *Dunf. Reg.*, no 39; JM Webster, 'The Lands of Masterton', in 'Notes on the Burgh of Dunfermline' (typescript, Dunfermline Carnegie Library, n.d.), 12.
5 *Dunf. Reg.*, no 1.
6 *Dunf. Reg.*, nos 1–26 deal largely with the king's endowments to the church. The Exchequer Rolls throughout the fourteenth and fifteenth, and even into the sixteenth centuries reinforce how important these endowments were to the abbey (*ER*, ii, iii, iv, v, vi, vii, viii and ix, *passim*), as do the various acts of later kings, eg *The Charters of King David I: the written acts of David I King of Scots, 1124–53, and of his son Henry Earl of Northumberland, 1139–52*, ed. GWS Barrow (Woodbridge, 1999), 62 (nos 17 and 18), 63 (nos 19, 20, 21 and 22) and *passim*; *RRS*, iv, *passim*; *RRS*, v, *passim*; *RRS*, vi, *passim*.
7 *Dunf. Reg.*, no 26.
8 J Masterton, 'A study of growth patterns and changing cultural landscapes of a Scottish town' (Unpublished typescript, Dunfermline Carnegie Library).
9 *Androw of Wyntoun, the Orygynale Cronykil of Scotland*, ed. D Laing (*The Historians of Scotland*, ii (Edinburgh, 1872–97)), bk vii, ch i, fo 156b.

10 J Froissart, *Chronicles of England, France, Spain, Portugal, Brittany, Flanders and the adjoining countries,* from the French by J Fournier, Lord Berners. Reprinted from Pynson's edition of 1523 and 1525 (1812), ii, 7.

11 *Dunf. Recs,* 304, 305 and 318.

12 *Dunf. Recs,* 126; *DGCB,* fo 29r.

13 *Dunf. Recs,* 45; NLS, Adv. Ms. 29-4-2, 'Huttons Collections', vi, fo 258; *Dunf. Recs,* 293.

14 *Dunf. Reg.,* no 370.

15 *Dunf. Recs,* 2, 157, 310, 97 and 99.

16 *Cal. Docs Scot.,* iv, 136.

17 *Cal. Docs Scot.,* iv, 459.

18 *DGCB,* fo 103r.

19 *Dunf. Recs,* 136.

20 *Calendar of Entries in the Papal Registers relating to Great Britain and Ireland: Papal Letters,* ed. JM Tremlow (London, 1933), xii, 297; J Wormald, *Court, Kirk and Community, Scotland 1470–1625* (London, 1981), 64.

21 Webster, 'Notes', 29.

22 *Dunf. Recs,* 160, 45, 105, 114, 138, 125, 65, 98, 194, 264 and 266; *DGCB,* fo 19v.

23 *Dunf. Recs,* 38 and 48; *DGCB, passim.*

24 *Dunf. Recs,* 160, 45, 105, 114, 138 and 125.

25 R Fawcett, *Medieval Abbeys and Churches of Fife; a Heritage Guide* (Fife Regional Council, n.d.), 16; S Boardman, 'Dunfermline as a Royal Mausoleum', in *Royal Dunfermline,* ed. R Fawcett (Edinburgh, 2005), 139–53.

26 A Mercer, *The History of Dunfermline from the Earliest Records to the Present Time* (Dunfermline, 1828), 55 and 56.

27 EP Dennison, ' Dunfermline Gild Court Book; missing folios', *Miscellany xiii* (SHS, 2004), 44.

28 *Dunf. Recs,* 62 and 157.

29 *DGCB,* fos 104v and 7v, for example.

30 *Dunf. Recs,* 319 and 334.

31 *DGCB,* fo 108v.

32 *DGCB,* fo 4r.

33 NAS, B20/1/1 (Protocol Book of John Cunninghame 1556/7–76), 104r; *Dunf. Recs,* 11, 297, 113, 360, 77 and 297.

34 *Dunf. Reg.,* no 370.

35 IB Cowan and DE Easson (eds), *Medieval Religious Houses: Scotland* (Glasgow, 1964), 175.

36 *RMS,* iv, nos 2514, 2969.

37 *Dunf. Recs,* 2 and 341.

38 Henderson, *Annals,* 323.

39 Henderson, *Annals,* 95.

40 J Fernie, *A History of the Town and Parish of Dunfermline* (Dunfermline, 1815), 47.

41 Archives of the Earl of Elgin and Kincardine, temporary reference 46/278.

42 *Dunf. Recs,* p. xxix.

43 *Dunf. Recs,* 267.

44 *RMS,* v, no 736.

45 J Grant, *History of the Burgh Schools of Scotland* (London and Glasgow, 1876), 64.

46 EP Dennison Torrie, 'The Gild of Dunfermline in the Fifteenth Century' (Unpublished PhD thesis, University of Edinburgh, 1984), 322.

47 *Dunf. Recs,* 323 and 336.

48 *Dunf. Recs,* 304.

49 *Dunf. Recs,* 77 and 99; *DGCB,* fos 21v and 34r, for example.

50 *Dunf. Recs,* 113; *DGCB,* fo 99v.

51 E Beveridge, *Viagraphia Dunfermlyensis* (Dunfermline, 1827, revised 1858), 38.

52 NAS, RH2/1/76 (a transcript of B20/1/1), (Protocol Book of John Cunynghame, 1556/7 – 76), fo 12, 22 October 1557.

53 *Dunf. Recs,* 317, 8, 80, 113, 154, 298, 172, 276 and 278.

54 *DGCB,* fo 24v.

55 *Dunf. Recs,* 75; *DGCB,* fo 104v.

56 *Dunf. Recs,*13.

57 *Dunf. Recs,* 51; *DGCB,* fo 8v.

58 *Dunf. Recs,* 349.

59 J Kirk, R Tanner and A Dunlop (eds), *Calendar of Scottish Supplications to Rome* (Edinburgh, 1997), v (1447–71), no 1322 (pp 395–6).

60 D Thomson, *The Dunfermline Hammermen; a History of the Incorporation of Hammermen in Dunfermline* (Paisley, 1909), *passim*; and D Thomson, *The Weavers' Craft, being a History of the Weavers' Incorporation of Dunfermline* (Paisley, 1903), *passim*, give details of two of the important crafts in the town.

61 *Dunf. Recs,* 345, 334, 86, 235, 208, 156, 337, 302 and 284.

62 *Dunf. Reg.,* no 596; Webster, 'Notes', 7.

63 *Dunf. Recs,* 230.

64 *DGCB,* fo 100v.

65 NAS, B20/1/2 (Protocol Book of David Brown, 1594–1612), 17.

66 *Dunf. Recs., passim.*

67 Webster, 'Notes', 27.

68 For further details of the old street pattern *see* Pitcairn, *'Fitpaths', passim;* and A Brotchie, *Wheels Around Dunfermline and Fife* (Catrine, n.d.)

69 DER Watt and N Shead, *The Heads of Religious Houses in Scotland from Twelfth to Fifteenth Centuries* (SRS, 2001), 71–3. For fuller details of the Pitcairn and Durie families and the Reformation, *see* M Dilworth, 'Dunfermline, Duries and the Reformation', *Scottish Church History Society Records,* 31 (2002), 37– 67.

70 *John Knox's History of the Reformation in Scotland,* ed. WC Dickinson, 2 vols (London, 1949), i, 276.

71 *DGCB,* fo 59r.

72 NAS, RH11/27/16, Regality of Dunfermline Register of Decreets, 1596–1610, 68 (7 May 1598).

73 M Dilworth, 'Monks and ministers after 1560', *Records of the Scottish Church History Society,* 18 (1974), 216–20; *RSS,* viii, no 2703.

74 Chalmers, *Account,* ii, 271; for details of royalty and important personages buried in the abbey and its graveyard, *see* S Pitcairn, *Dunfermline Abbey and Churchyard* (Edinburgh, 2003), *passim.*

75 Henderson, *Annals,* 205.

76 *RPC,* i:, 246 (13 September 1563); Webster, 'Notes', 31, gives details of responsibilities for the maintenance of the church.

77 Henderson, *Annals,* 213 and 216.

78 *Dunf. Reg.,* p. 476.

79 *Dunf. Reg.,* Appendix iii, pp. 465–504; Henderson, *Annals,* 215, 262, 263 and 264, for example.

80 Chalmers, *Account,* i, 159; *See also* J Fergusson, *The White Hind and Other Discoveries* (London, 1963), 55 and 56.

81 *APS,* iii, 438; *See also RSS,* iv, no 1987, and *RSS,* viii, nos 2384, 2434, 2514, 2533, 2538, 2553, 2572, 2588, 2703 and 2736.

82 *RMS,* vii, no 1572.

83 Henderson, *Annals,* 195.

84 *RMS,* v, no 1731, and vii, no 75; *APS,* iv, 23–4.

85 Henderson, *Annals,* 239–40.

86 F Grose, The *Antiquities of Scotland*, 2 vols (London, 1797), ii 121.

87 Henderson, *Annals*, 231.

88 Shearer, *Extracts*, 37.

89 Henderson, *Annals*, 264, 267 and 278.

90 Henderson, *Annals*, 264, 267 and 278.

91 Henderson, *Annals*, 267.

92 Chalmers, *Account*, i, 89; *Dunf. Reg.*, no 370.

93 *Accounts of the Master of Works*, eds HM Paton *et al* (Edinburgh, 1957–), ii, 29.

94 Chalmers, *Account*, i, 325. Others, such as G Pride in *The Kingdom of Fife: An Illustrated Archaeological Guide* (Royal Incorporation of Architects in Scotland, 1990), 13, suggest a later date of about 1635.

95 Chalmers, *Account*, i, 245.

96 Henderson, *Annals*, 281–2.

97 Shearer, *Extracts*, 7.

98 *TA*, ii, 463.

99 D Calderwood, *History of the Kirk of Scotland* (Wodrow Society, 1843), iv, 448–9; AS Cunningham, *Romantic Culross, Torryburn, Carnock, Cairneyhill, Saline and Pitfirrane* (Dunfermline, 1902), 124.

100 Shearer, *Extracts*, 20–23.

101 Shearer, *Extracts*, 49.

102 *RMS*, viii, no 2091; NAS, RH11/27/17 (Dunfermline Regality Register of Decreets, 1609–36), 55; RH11/27/18 (Dunfermline Regality Court Book, 1612–21), 21; RH11/27/17, 122 and 588; RH11/27/19 (Dunfermline Regality Court Book, 1669–80), 95.

103 NAS, RH11/27/16 (Dunfermline Regality Register of Decreets, 1596–1610), 225.

104 Henderson, *Annals*, 263.

105 Henderson, *Annals*, 292–3.

106 Henderson, *Annals*, 360.

107 NAS, RH11/27/15 (Dunfermline Regality Register of Decreets, 1591–1611), 303, 342 and 349.

108 Henderson, *Annals*, 265.

109 NAS, B20/1/2 (Protocol Book of David Brown, 1594–1612), 18 and 62, for example.

110 Shearer, *Extracts*, 4.

111 Shearer, *Extracts*, 42, for example.

112 *Dunf. Recs*, 360 and 103, for example; NAS, B20/1/2 (Protocol Book of David Brown, 1594–1612), 73 and 128, for example.

113 R J Naismith, *Buildings of the Scottish Countryside* (London, 1985), 21–2.

114 Bert McEwan, pers comm.

115 Henderson, *Annals*, 248.

116 Chalmers, *Account*, ii, 304; cf NAS RH11/27/17, 479.

117 NAS, B20/1/4 (Protocol Book of Henry Elder, 1656–61), fo 6r (27 December 1656).

118 NAS, B20/1/3 (Protocol Book of Johne Auchinwallis, 1642–50), fo 11 (15 May 1643) and fo 17 (17 January 1644).

119 Henderson, *Annals*, 290–91.

120 Henderson, *Annals*, 301.

121 NAS, CH2/592/1/1 (Dunfermline Kirk Session Records, 1640–89), 6 February 1649.

122 NAS, CH2/592/1/1, 72.

123 NAS, CH2/592/1/1, 9 (26 January 1641), 63 (7 December 1647), 137 (26 July 1653), 140 (8 November 1653), 141(22 November 1653), 147 (8 August 1654); CH2/592/2, 11(22 October 1701); CH2/592/3, 84 (22 February 1711) and 88 (15 March 1711), for example.

124 NAS, CH2/592/1/1, 6, 13, 15, 22, 24, 25 and *passim*, for example.

125 Henderson, *Annals*, 296, 298, 310 and 300.

126 NAS, CH2/592/1/1, 54 (25 April 1647).

127 NAS, CH2/592/1/1, 17, 24 (31 July 1655).

128 Henderson, *Annals*, 342 and 344.

129 NAS, CH2/592/1/1, 29 October 1643.

130 NAS, CH2/592/1/1, 9 March 1641.

131 NAS, CH2/592/1/1, 10 (23 February 1641).

132 NAS, CH2/592/1/1, 17 April 1660.

133 Henderson, *Annals*, 354 and 377.

134 NAS, CH2/592/1/1, 4 April 1643.

135 J Wilkie, *Bygone Fife* (Edinburgh, 1931), 14.

136 Henderson, *Annals*, 316–17.

137 NAS, CH2/592/1/1, 29 March 1653; 20 April 1658.

138 Shearer, *Extracts*, 12.

139 Shearer, *Extracts*, 25.

140 *APS*, viii, 90.

141 NAS, CH2/592/1/1, 17 July 1651; 30 September 1651.

142 Henderson, *Annals*, 338.

143 Henderson, *Annals*, 366.

144 *Geological Survey of Scotland* (1928 edn), 'Fifeshire Western Division', sheet xxxviii, NE.

145 NAS, B20/10/4 (Dunfermline Burgh Council Minutes, 1619–32), 24 April 1624; Dunfermline Burgh Records – per Rev JM Webster 'The Lands of Baldridge' (typescript, Dunfermline Carnegie Library), 11. For further information on coal seams in the locality see, Chalmers, *Account*, i, 311–320.

146 Henderson, *Annals*, 343.

147 T Hunter, *Mining in West Fife: the Crossgates Area, in particular Fordell and Halbeath Collieries* (Norwich, 2001), *passim*.

148 *Dunf. Reg.*, nos 332, 218–19.

149 NAS B20/13/2 (Dunfermline Burgh Council Minutes, 1662–81), 18 April 1668.

150 NAS B20/13/3 (Dunfermline Burgh Council Minutes, 1692–1711), 27 May 1700.

151 WT Barr, *For a Web Begun: the Story of Dunfermline* (Edinburgh, 1947), 24.

152 Henderson, *Annals*, 356.

153 NAS, E69/10/1 (Hearth Tax, Dunfermline); cf EP Dennison and R Coleman, *Historic Linlithgow* (Scottish Burgh Survey, 2000), 35; and EP Dennison and R Coleman, *Historic Musselburgh* (Scottish Burgh Survey, 1996), 34.

154 'Register containing the State and Condition of Every Burgh within the Kingdom of Scotland, in the Year 1692', in *Miscellany of the Scottish Burgh Records Society* (Edinburgh, 1881), 112–13.

155 Henderson, *Annals*, 370.

156 NAS, B20/13/4 (Dunfermline Burgh Council Minutes, 1696–1726), 22 August 1702.

157 NAS, B20/13/4, May 1705; 9 April 1718.

158 NAS, B20/13/4, 18 October 1752.

159 NAS, B20/13/4, 4 November 1754.

160 NAS B20/13/10 (Dunfermline Burgh Council Minutes, 1762–69), 30 November 1765.

161 Henderson, *Annals*, 374.

162 NAS, B20/13/4, 1 July 1710.

163 Henderson, *Annals*, 519.

164 'A View of the Town of Dunfermline, with the situation and distance of the [—]
from the said town, surveyed and delineated in the year 1766 by [—]' (1766 map),
in Dunfermline Carnegie Library, Local History Room.

165 Henderson, *Annals*, 428.

166 NAS, B20/13/7 (Dunfermline Burgh Council Minutes, 1739–45), 8 December
1739.

167 1766 map.

168 NAS, B20/13/8 (Dunfermline Burgh Council Minutes, 1745–54), 11 January
1752.

169 NAS, B20/13/8, 2 May 1752; 16 May 1752; 10 April 1754; NAS, B20/13/10
(Dunfermline Burgh Council Minutes, 1762–9), 6 August 1763.

170 1766 map.

171 NAS, B20/13/8, 28 June 1753.

172 NAS, B20/13/10, 14 April 1764; 1766 map.

173 NAS, B20/13/10, 16 November 1765, 4 January 1766, 15 January 1766, 17
January 1766 etc, *passim* through to 9 May 1769; *OSA*, x, 274–5.

174 Henderson, *Annals*, 492.

175 *OSA*, x, 275

176 Dunfermline Carnegie Library (DLC/Pal), MS, Library of Erskine Beveridge,
'The Lord Appellant against James Hunt, Respondent', n.p.

177 1766 map.

178 Henderson, *Annals*, 486.

179 NAS, B20/13/10, 27 July 1769.

180 Henderson, *Annals*, 510.

181 Henderson, *Annals*, 492 and 494.

182 Henderson, *Annals*, 499.

183 NAS, B20/13/13, 5 January 1793.

184 Drawn by Robert Scotland for George Chalmers.

185 The 1766 map suggests that the east end of High Street was called
'Horsemarket'.

186 Typescript, 'Closes' by B McEwan (2006); Henderson, *Annals*, 515, 517, 628, 629
and 707.

187 Henderson, *Annals*, 668.

188 McEwan, 'Closes'.

189 NAS, B20/13/6 (Dunfermline Burgh Council Minutes, 1728–35), 7 October
1730.

190 NAS, B20/13/13 (Dunfermline Burgh Council Minutes, 1784–96), August 1790.

191 Henderson, *Annals*, 523.

192 NAS, B20/13/7 (Dunfermline Burgh Council Minutes, 1739–45), 17 January
1741.

193 NAS, B20/13/8 (Dunfermline Burgh Council Minutes, 1745–54), 16 July 1751.

194 NAS, B20/13/9 (Dunfermline Burgh Council Minutes, 1754–62), 56.

195 Henderson, *Annals*, 487–8.

196 McEwan, *Dunfermline: Our Heritage*, *passim*, gives details of the many historic
buildings in and around the town.

197 NAS, B20/13/11 (Dunfermline Burgh Council Minutes, 1769–76), 16 November
1771 and 31 December 1771; Henderson, *Annals*, 494.

198 NAS, B20/13/13, 27 August 1791; 30 March 1793.

199 NAS, B20/13/4 (Dunfermline Burgh Council Minutes, 1696–1726), 22 March
1701; NAS, B20/13/7 (Dunfermline Burgh Council Minutes, 1739–45),
11 September 1740.

200 NAS, B20/13/8, 18 October 1752.

201 NAS, B20/13/10, 17 July 1765.

202 Henderson, *Annals*, 502 and 469.

203 NAS, B20/13/4, 14 November 1702; 28 November 1713.

204 NAS, B20/13/11, 17 April 1773.

205 NAS, B20/13/13, 16 May 1786.

206 NAS, B20/13/13, 16 March 1787.

207 NAS, B20/13/9, 56.

208 Henderson, *Annals*, 421.

209 NAS, B20/13/11, 15 April 1772; Henderson, *Annals*, 517.

210 Henderson, *Annals*, 370.

211 NAS, B20/13/9, 3 May 1758 and 25 March 1758.

212 RT Millar, 'Water Supply: a Short Historical Note' (typescript, Dunfermline Carnegie Library, Local History Room, 1966, D/MUN Wat).

213 NAS, B20/13/8, 26 May 1750.

214 Henderson, *Annals*, 528 and 532.

215 Henderson, *Annals*, 420–21 and 510.

216 A Shearer, 'Notes on Minute Book for the Dean of Guild Court of Dunfermline, begun 20 February 1753 and ending 15 July 1778' (Dunfermline, 1773) (Dunfermline Carnegie Library), 4, 5–6.

217 Chalmers, *Account*, i, 99.

218 Henderson, *Annals*, 397.

219 NAS, CH2/592/2 (Dunfermline Kirk Session Records, 1701–06), 47 (9 March 1704) and 49 (20 April 1704); CH/592/3 (Dunfermline Kirk Session Records, 1706–15), 107 (28 June 1711) and 109 (5 July 1711).

220 NAS, CH2/592/5 (Dunfermline Kirk Session Records, 1725–34), 11 September 1728; Henderson, *Annals*, 431.

221 NAS, B20/13/6, 23 and 29 November 1734.

222 NAS, B20/13/7 (Dunfermline Burgh Council Minutes, 1739–45), 7 March 1743 and 15 September 1744.

223 Henderson, *Annals*, 485.

224 Henderson, *Annals*, 436.

225 Henderson, *Annals*, 465.

226 Henderson, *Annals*, 477.

227 Chalmers, *Account*, ii, 320.

228 *Dunfermline City Trail*.

229 Henderson, *Annals*, 469, 506 and 538.

230 Henderson, *Annals*, 513 and 585.

231 Henderson, *Annals*, 475.

232 Henderson, *Annals*, 400.

233 NAS, B20/13/6 (Dunfermline Burgh Council Minutes, 1728–35), 9 July 1731, 7 March 1735 and 21 March 1735.

234 NAS, B20/13/7, 18 February 1744.

235 Henderson, *Annals*, 450.

236 NAS, B20/13/9, 11 October 1758; Henderson, *Annals*, 473 and 487.

237 NAS, B20/13/8, 9 May 1752.

238 Henderson, *Annals*, 512.

239 'MS Guild Merchant Records, 1586–1770', in possession of Dunfermline Guildry, 11 October 1718.

240 NAS, B20/13/8, 3 March 1753.

241 R Pococke, *Tours In Scotland* (SHS, 1887), 287.

242 *OSA*, x, 273.

243 D Thomson (1832–1908), 'Anent Dunfermline, Manuscript Notes Antiquarian and Contemporary', vol i, 37; Henderson, *Annals*, 528.

244 R Heron, *Scotland Delineated* (Edinburgh, 1975, originally published 1791), 179.

245 NAS, B20/13/6, 26 Dec 1732 and 22 January 1733.

246 Henderson, *Annals*, 434.

247 NAS, B20/13/7, 4 August 1739.

248 NAS, B20/13/9, 41, 85, 51 and 64.

249 NAS, B20/13/9, 7 January 1760.

250 Henderson, *Annals*, 487.

251 T Pennant, *A Tour in Scotland and Voyage to the Hebrides* (Edinburgh, 1998, originally published 1772), pt II, vol iii, 212–13.

252 NAS, B20/13/7, 20 August 1740.

253 Henderson, *Annals*, 505, 511 and 519.

254 Henderson, *Annals*, 502.

255 NAS, B20/13/9, 352.

256 NAS, B20/13/10, 18 June 1763, for example.

257 NAS, B20/13/10, 6 August 1763, 14 April 1764, 26 October 1764, 26 January 1765, 2 February 1765, 4 March 1765, 9 April 1765, 3 June 1765, 17 July 1765, 13 August 1765, 3 September 1765, 20 November 1765, 13 June 1766, 24 January 1767 and 11 June 1768.

258 Henderson, *Annals*, 483; Miller, 'Water Supply: A Short Historical Note' gives further details.

259 NAS, B20/13/11 (Dunfermline Burgh Council Minutes, 1769–76), 28 May 1773.

260 NAS, B20/13/4, 9 January 1721; NAS, B20/13/9, 4 October 1760; and NAS, B20/13/13, 10 May 1785.

261 NAS, RH11/27/16 (Dunfermline Regality Register of Decreets, 1596–1610), 251.

262 NAS, B20/13/4, 7 June 1704 and 30 May 1710.

263 Thomson, *Dunfermline Hammermen*, 229 and 231.

264 *OSA*, x, 289; Henderson, *Annals*, 417, 440, 481 and 487.

265 NAS, B20/13/8, 16 June 1752, 16 September 1752 and 21 September 1754.

266 NAS, E326/1/42, 'Window Tax, Fife County', 1748.

267 Henderson, *Annals*, 501.

268 *OSA*, x, 289; Henderson, *Annals*, 396, 520, 534 and 536.

269 Henderson, *Annals*, 547.

270 NAS, B20/13/14 (Dunfermline Burgh Court Minutes, 1796–1807), 21 June 1802.

271 Henderson, *Annals*, 551.

272 Pitcairn, 'Fitpaths', 333.

273 Henderson, *Annals*, 608, 610 and 628.

274 NAS, B20/13/14, 3 January, 1807.

275 Henderson, *Annals*, 564.

276 *Dunfermline Saturday Press and West of Fife Advertiser*, 14 July and 1 September 1877; *Dunfermline Journal*, 14 July and 1 September 1877.

277 Henderson, *Annals*, 668.

278 Henderson, *Annals*, 702–03.

279 Henderson, *Annals*, 568, 569 and 620–21.

280 Henderson, *Annals*, 600; Pitcairn, 'Fitpaths', 233–4.

281 For full details, *see* Henderson, *Annals*, 570–75.

282 Henderson, *Annals*, 555, 556 and 566.

283 H Walker, *The Story of Erskine Beveridge and St Leonard's Works, 1833–1989* (Dunfermline, 1991) gives fuller details of the town's mills; Thomson, 'Anent Dunfermline', vol ix, item 270.

284 Thomson, 'Anent Dunfermline', vol iv, item 487.

285 A Gardner, pers comm; Thomson, 'Anent Dunfermline', vol ix, item 362.

286 Henderson, *Annals*, 678.

287 Chalmers, *Account*, ii, 63–5; E Beveridge *Viagraphy Dunfermlynensis* (Dunfermline, 1827, revised 1858), 252.

288 Henderson, *Annals*, 707.

289 Henderson, *Annals*, 706.

290 NAS, B20/13/15 (Dunfermline Burgh Council Minutes, 1807–12), 17 July 1807.

291 Chalmers, *Account*, i, 393–4.

292 Henderson, *Annals*, 669.

293 *Dunfermline Press*, 21 August 1869.

294 R Fawcett, *The Abbey and Palace of Dunfermline* (Historic Scotland, 1990), 28.

295 Thomson, 'Anent Dunfermline', vol i, 114.

296 Thomson,' Anent Dunfermline', vol i, item 133.

297 Henderson, *Annals*, 579, 695 and 700.

298 Pitcairn,'*Fitpaths*', 338.

299 B McEwan, pers comm.

300 H Walker, *The Story of Erskine Beveridge and St Leonard's Works, 1833–1989* (Carnegie Dunfermline Trust, 1991), 13.

301 Henderson, *Annals*, 588, 593, 590, 650, 676, 681, 704 and 671.

302 R Somerville, *Dunfermline Sketches and Notes* (Dunfermline, 1917), section xix.

303 Henderson, *Annals*, 617, 624, 634, 649 and 658.

304 Henderson, *Annals*, 852.

305 McEwan, *Dunfermline: Our Heritage*, 10.

306 Henderson, *Annals*, 549, 575, 554, 580 and 704.

307 Chalmers, *Account*, i, 386–8.

308 A J Warden, *The Linen Trade, Ancient and Modern* (London, 1864), 554–8 gives an overview of the linen trade

309 Henderson, *Annals*, 585.

310 Henderson, *Annals*, 590.

311 Chalmers, *Account*, i, 396.

312 Henderson, *Annals*, 613 and 631.

313 Henderson, *Annals*, 641.

314 Walker, *Story of Erskine Beveridge*, 9–10.

315 Walker, *Story of Erskine Beveridge* gives further details.

316 H Walker, *The History of Hay and Robertson Ltd and the Robertson Family of Dunfermline* (Carnegie Dunfermline Trust, 1996), 5.

317 Walker, *The History of Hay and Robertson*, 3 and 7.

318 Walker, *The History of Hay and Robertson*, 7 and 5.

319 Henderson, *Annals*, 585, 586 and 641.

320 Ronald Watt, pers comm.

321 E Simpson, *The Auld Grey Toun: Dunfermline in the Time of Andrew Carnegie* (Dunfermline, 1987*)*, 11.

322 Simpson, *Auld Grey Toun*, 36 and 39.

323 Henderson, *Annals*, 585, 586, 641 and 666.

324 Henderson, *Annals*, 552, 590 and 687.

325 Simpson, *Auld Grey Toun*, 11.

326 PP, xvii, 'Annual Reports of the Inspectors of Mines' in *Reports from Commissioners, Inspectors and Others to Parliament, 1876*.

327 Henderson, *Annals*, 642.

328 R Watt, 'History of Coal Mining Round Dunfermline', appendix, p 12 (Unpublished typescript, 1999, Dunfermline Carnegie Library). See also M Oglethorpe, *Scottish Collieries: an inventory of Scotland's coal industry in the nationalised era* (Edinburgh, 2006) on Dunfermline and surroundings.

329 Henderson, *Annals*, 578 and 648. For a more detailed and accurate account, see A Brotchie and H Jack, *The Early Railways of Fife* (forthcoming, 2007).

330 Thomson, 'Anent Dunfermline', vol i, items 509, 938.

331 Thomson, 'Anent Dunfermline', vol i, item 152.

332 Henderson, *Annals*, 570 and 694.

333 14 Park Avenue, deeds.

334 A Stewart, *Reminiscences of Dunfermline* (Dunfermline, 1886), 7.

335 Simpson, *Auld Grey Toun*, 11.

336 Henderson, *Annals*, 651.

337 *Dunfermline Advertiser*, 12 October 1849.

338 'Letter from James Anson to James Hunt of Pittencrieff', Dunfermline Carnegie Library, Local History Room.

339 Thomson, 'Anent Dunfermline', vol i, item 238.

340 Thomson, 'Anent Dunfermline', vol i, items 501 and 938; vol iii, items 480 and 520; vol vi, items 269 and 311. *See also* NAS, B20/13/9, 226.

341 Thomson, 'Anent Dunfermline', vol i, item 938.

342 Henderson, *Annals*, 618 and 622.

343 Henderson, *Annals*, 635, 645 and 667.

344 *OSA*, x, 277.

345 *Dunfermline Advertiser*, 17 August 1849.

346 Henderson, *Annals*, 663 and 706.

347 Millennium Project, 'Twentieth-Century Dunfermline', *passim*.

348 P Geddes, *City Development, a Study of Parks, Gardens and Culture-Institutes: a Report to the Carnege Dunfermline Trust* (Dunfermline, 1904).

349 Geddes, *City Development*, 90, 83–8 and 148–52, for example.

350 Geddes, *City Development*, 21–4.

Pittencrieff house

Plates

1 W Roy's Military Survey
1747–55

2 St Leonard's Chapel,
by E Galloway
(courtesy of Fife Council
Dunfermline Museum)

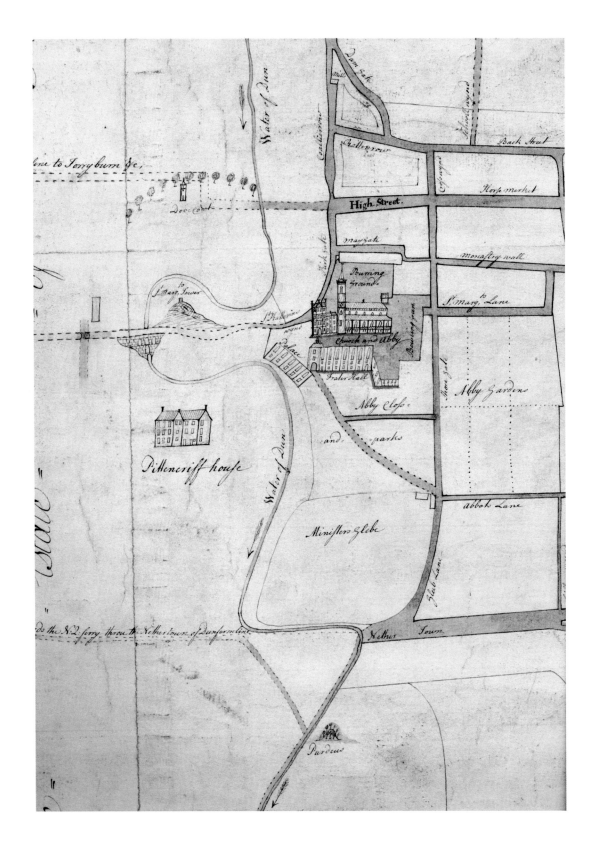

line to Torryburn &c.

Water of Den

Dam Dyke

Mill

Coulsnacoss

Dovecoat

Rattenrow

Back Street

Copingate

Horse market

High Street

Kirkgate

maygate

monastry wall

St Marg Tower

St Katherine wynd

Burning ground

St Mary to Lane

Church and Abby

Bowling green

Rotten gate

Palace

Frater Hall

Abby Close

Abby Gardens

Pittencrieff house

Water of Den

and parks

Minister Glebe

Abbots Lane

Glab Lane

to the N:Q: ferry throu the Nethertown of Dunfermline

Nether Town

Purdeus

4 Dovecot in Pittencrieff or St Lawrence Yard, by A Campbell (courtesy of Dunfermline Heritage Trust, Forrester Collection)

5 View of Dunfermline from Heugh Mills, illustrator unknown (courtesy of Dunfermline Heritage Trust, Forrester Collection)

3 left Section from 1766 map (courtesy of Dunfermline Carnegie Library)

6 Nether-gate
(Nether Yett) of abbey
in 2006

7 92 St Margaret Street
(courtesy of Alan Calder)

8 Kinnis Court,
by A Westwood
(courtesy of
Dunfermline Carnegie
Library)

9 View of Dunfermline
from the north-west,
by W H Paton
(courtesy of Fife Council
Dunfermline Museum)

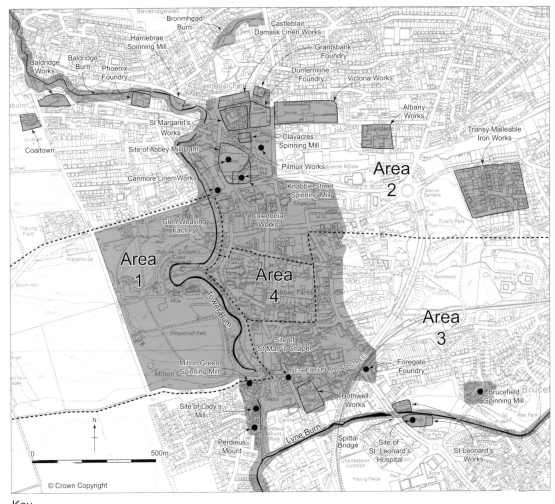

Key

known archaeological potential

10 Areas of prime archaeological interest
(Reproduced by permission of Ordnance Survey on behalf of HMSO. © Crown Copyright 2007.
All rights reserved. Ordnance Survey Licence Number 100013329)

Consult Fife Council's Archaeological Unit on development both within and outside this area.

The boundaries of the areas discussed below are shown in **plate 10**, which also includes sites mentioned in the text outside the central part of Dunfermline. Sites and locations within the boundaries of the burgh and abbey are shown in **figures 34 and 35**.

The category of listed buildings is correct in 2007. Category may be subject to change in future.

Area 1: Pittencrieff Glen and west of Tower Burn

The mansion of Pittencrieff House and surrounding designed landscape of Pittencrieff Park dominate Area 1. The Park includes lawns, flowerbeds and the wooded glen of the Tower Burn. The Glen has traditionally defined the western boundary of the town and has a romantic character **plate 9**. It contains monuments associated with some iconic figures of Scottish history.

Malcolm Canmore's Tower

The ruins on Tower Hill (a Scheduled Ancient Monument and Category A-listed) **figure 34** have been associated with King Malcolm since they were first recorded in the seventeenth century and a fifteenth-century reference to 'Tower Burn' must mean the tower had been built by that time.[1] The Scottish Urban Archaeological Trust (SUAT) confirmed the tower's medieval origins during an excavation in 1988.[2] They excavated an area within the surviving L-shaped foundations and recovered pottery that suggested the tower had been in use during the fourteenth and fifteenth centuries. More precisely, an iron coin punch retrieved during nineteenth-century excavations has been attributed to David II (1329–71).[3] All this dating evidence suggests that the tower might have been built during the Wars of Independence. The SUAT excavation also recorded some evidence of earlier quarrying, presumably for sandstone, on the summit of the hill.[4] The quarrying may have removed remains of an earlier fortification, although there was nothing to suggest that one had been there in the first place. The excavator's interpretation was that the substantial foundations must have supported a strong tower that protected the town's western approach and the Wars of Independence were a likely motivation for its construction.[5] The oval wall that surrounds the site today is much later in date and has nothing to do with the medieval remains.

An interesting array of artefacts was found during landscaping works on the slopes around the tower in 1905–06. Not surprisingly, the inhabitants of the tower had disposed of rubbish by tipping it over the surrounding cliffs and the landscaping work turned up bones and pottery, as well as the more surprising find of a fossil from a large reptile.[6] Looking at the slopes today it is important to remember that they have been completely refaced following this landscaping.[7]

Caves and wells in Pittencrieff Glen

There are some caves in the sides of the Glen and the most famous is that traditionally associated with Queen Margaret **figures 21 and 34**. This small cave contains benches carved out of the rock along both sides and a well toward the rear.[8] These features are not clearly visible today and the cave is now located at the end of a modern subterranean passage beneath the Bridge Street Car Park. Nobody knows at what date the cave was created and there do not seem to have been any modern excavations in or around it.

There was a notice of another cave uncovered on the north side of Tower Hill during landscaping works in 1905–06.[9] Apparently this cave contained a crude fireplace and ashes. This presumably was one of the two caves still apparent and close together on the north side of the hill **figure 34**.

These caves are much altered from their original form and, without the benefit of modern excavation, are difficult to interpret. They may have been hermitages for the abbey monks and could presumably have been used for religious devotion, although they are not in the most isolated of locations.

The 'Spa Well' was recorded as an antiquity in the mid nineteenth century, when it was known as the 'Spaw Well' or 'Well of Spaw'.[10] It was traditionally associated with the name of Wallace but it is not known when this association came about. It is drystone built and survives within the Park **figure 34**. It is impossible to say anything more about it without further archaeological investigation but historical research confirms that the well was in use in the later eighteenth century (*see* p 50).

Possible site of the early burgh

The early history of the town is obscure and a grant by David I to the abbey, which refers to his burgh of Dunfermline as being 'on this side of the water (or 'nearer side of the water') in which the monastery is situated' (*see* p 15) has been taken as implying that there may have been settlement on both sides of the Tower Burn.[11] As none is apparent on the west side of the burn today it has been assumed that any such settlement, if it existed, must have failed and been replaced by one which developed beside the abbey.[12] No archaeological trace of any such settlement has been found.

Aerial photography has recorded some linear markings on the lawns in Pittencrieff Park and a geophysical survey was undertaken to investigate whether the marks corresponded to buried walls or filled ditches **figure 34**.[13] The survey did record some features that may be significant but nothing that was likely to have related to a medieval settlement. The only artefacts that have been found in the Park have come from around known monuments such as Tower Hill, despite much landscaping having been undertaken. Given the lack of physical evidence, and the lack of clarity as to exactly what this charter is referring to, the case for an early settlement on the west side of the Tower Burn must be viewed with caution. It should be noted that very early in the medieval period there are two distinct settlements associated with the abbey, namely Dunfermline itself and Netherton (*see* pp 15–16).

Pittencrieff Park designed landscape

Sir Alexander Clerk gave instructions for Pittencrieff Mansion to be built in 1610.[14] An extra floor was added in 1731[15] an early depiction of which can be seen on a perspective view surveyed in 1766 **plate 3**.[16] Andrew Carnegie purchased the house in 1903[17] and in 1911 Robert Lorimer undertook renovation work. The Category A-listed mansion is now home to historical displays and exhibitions **figure 34**.[18] The grounds contain some interesting structures such as a late eighteenth-century doocot, which is Category B-listed **figure 34**.[19] A perhaps older doocot once stood in the southeast of the Park **plate 4**; it was marked 'Old Dove Cot' on the Ordnance Survey town plan surveyed in 1855 **figure 34**, but no surface trace of it remains.

The main western approach to the medieval town ran through the Park, passing over the burn in the same location as the current Tower Bridge **figure 34**, much as shown on Roy's map of 1747–55 **plate 1**. The current Category B-listed bridge consists of two levels of arches **figure 18**.[20] It contains a date stone inscribed 1788 and an inset date stone, presumably from the bridge it replaced, bearing the initials 'A R' and the date 1611.[21] A view created in 1766 **plate 3** shows the earlier bridge as consisting of three levels of arches. It has been suggested that there was a medieval bridge here from an early date because of a reference dated to 1327.[22]

Pittencrieff Park is listed in the Inventory of Historic Gardens and Designed Landscapes and is rated as 'outstanding' in terms of architectural and historical interest.[23] Due to the presence of the Park, this area has not seen the industrial development and modern housing growth that other parts of the town have sustained. Modern housing does extend up to the Park's northern and southern borders, however.

Area 2: north of the abbey precinct

A general north to south slope runs through the town. The main medieval streets developed along terraces that run east to west across it. Not surprisingly, High Street occupies the broadest terrace but the medieval owners of properties running back from the street still had to adapt to building and working on fairly steep inclines. The same is true of those properties on the west side of St Catherine's Wynd/ Kirkgate, which sloped down to Tower Burn.

West end of the town

It has been suggested that the first street in the upper township of Dunfermline may have been St Catherine's Wynd/Kirkgate.[24] This is possible but, if so, it appears that only the west side of the street was considered suitable for division into plots. On the first Ordnance Survey town plans, surveyed in 1855, it is clear that the plots on the east side are much shorter than those on the west. This is because the eastern plots are constrained by properties running south from High Street and they are likely to have been created at a later date than those on High Street. Protocol books make it clear that there were established tenements on the east side by the seventeenth century at the latest.[25] Those on the west have a typical medieval form and extend down to Tower Burn. The stream would have been a desirable feature to have at the rear of a medieval property and ready access to water would have been essential for many activities such as tanning or dyeing.

Medieval plots ran north from High Street to Queen Anne Street, which originated as a back lane to these properties. The western part of Queen Anne Street was formerly called 'Ratten Row' as marked on Wood's plan of 1823 **figure 4**. The derivation of this street name is likely to be the old Scots word 'rattan' or 'ratton' (*see* p 35) which referred to undressed timber and row implies that only one side of the street was lined with houses.[26]

By measuring the widths of properties in medieval towns it is sometimes apparent that they form blocks of similar size, although care must be taken because amalgamation and subdivision of plots was common. It is presumed that any obvious change in width between blocks of plots tells us that they were laid out at different times. It is often useful to measure widths on the first edition Ordnance Survey plans as these precede modern development. It can also help to measure the widths of surviving older properties on the ground to provide accuracy. From using both these techniques it seems that the original width of properties on the west side of Kirkgate was around six metres, for example at nos 17–19 Kirkgate **figure 34**. This value is typical of a medieval town and similar to some widths seen in Perth (of around five metres).[27] It also appears to be around the same value as plots at the west end of High Street, for example at nos 7–9 High Street **figure 34**.

Further east, beyond the line of Cross Wynd and Guildhall Street, the width of most plots appears to increase, although the smallest examples still remain around six metres. This general increase may reflect that these plots were laid out at a later date, as may the existence of Cross Wynd itself, as vennels were frequently formed along the former limits of a town.[28] We know that the west side of Cross Wynd was developed in 1489 (*see* p 18) so it was certainly an established feature by that time. It is also interesting to note that the plots on the north side of High Street are generally wider than those to the south. This may reflect that these properties are much shorter, rather than created at a different date, as it would be very unlikely that one side of High Street was laid out before the other.

Taking all these trends together, it would seem that the restricted width of plots at the west end of the town probably reflects that this was the most populated area. It also seems likely that the plots on the west side of Kirkgate and those at the west end of High Street were the first to be laid out. As the name implies, Kirkgate was probably an important route into the abbey and this end of town may have been the obvious location to create the first properties.

Archaeologists monitoring the excavation of service trenches along Kirkgate/St Catherine's Wynd **figure 34** have confirmed that interesting deposits do survive, at least in the south of the street. Unfortunately these works were limited and have added no information concerning the date the roadway was created.[29]

A more informative excavation was undertaken next to Wilson's Close in 1988 **figure 34**.[30] A trench was dug through up to two metres of archaeological deposits, which presumably accumulated here because the site lay at the foot of a steep slope from High Street. The deposits contained thirteenth-century pottery and at the base of the trench was clay containing organic material. The survival of organic materials, such as wood and leather, is extremely important because these normally decay very quickly. Only in special conditions, such as when kept constantly wet, will items such as shoes survive. Objects made from organic materials were probably more common than any other, but we know very little about them and any preservation is of exceptional interest. Dunfermline is built on clay, which retains water, and this means it has a better chance of having permanently wet deposits that preserve organic material than many other towns.[31]

The most important excavation yet undertaken in the town ran from 1988 to 1994 inside and around Abbot House before it was turned into a Heritage Centre **figure 34**.[32] The results suggested that in the medieval period the majority of the site was within the abbey precinct and these aspects are dealt with as part of Area 4 (*see* pp 116–17). However, some early features suggested that Maygate had originated as a narrow pathway between the edge of burgage plots and the precinct boundary.[33] The earliest pottery found in the plots dated to the twelfth century. It was not clear from the excavated evidence whether these plots stretched south from High Street or west from Kirkgate.[34] However, given the analysis of the town plan discussed above, it is suggested that the excavations uncovered the back wall of plots extending south from High Street.

The narrow path was expanded to become a metalled street in the thirteenth century and subsequent road surfaces interleaved with accumulations of midden were recorded.[35] The latest of these layers dated to the sixteenth century. The excavator suggested that the road was created to lead to an entrance into the abbey precinct at the east end of Maygate.[36] Although this excavation uncovered only a small area, it has confirmed that the plots at the west end of High Street were created as early as the twelfth century.

Archaeologists also monitored excavations as the town centre was pedestrianised in 1991 and 1992 **figure 34**.[37] Natural subsoil was noted directly beneath modern make-up in the majority of the trenches that were excavated. A sandstone conduit was noted in one trench but unfortunately nothing was found to date it. At least one possible pit, containing the remains of many leather shoes, was noted in another trench.[38] These observations confirm that preservation of archaeological deposits is generally less favoured as the slope the town sits on rises to the north. However, they also confirm that features cut into the subsoil do survive and any terracing will probably not have extended below the level of subsoil. It should be assumed that, even where modern development has cleared overlying archaeological deposits, important cut features such as pits, post-holes and drains would still survive. These features are likely to contain artefacts that will help date development of the town and tell us the trades of former inhabitants. The survival of a pit containing shoes in the town centre is noteworthy and suggests that features elsewhere could contain preserved organic material which, as noted above, is archaeologically rare (*see* p 81).

The plots on the west side of Bruce Street (formerly called Collier Row) are also medieval in form, although the original layout is difficult to ascertain even on the first Ordnance Survey town plan. Two excavations, which recovered medieval pottery towards the rear of nos 29–35 Bruce Street **figure 34**, have confirmed the large amount of post-medieval development in this part of town but also the potential for medieval remains.[39]

On Roy's map created in the eighteenth century an open lade seems to be depicted running along the east side of Bruce Street **plate 1**. On the map the lade appears to carry on to the south and east where it may have become the feature known as the 'Tron Burn'. Roy's map may also show 'The Goat', another open watercourse that led water away from the Mill Dam to the Tower Burn, which was marked clearly on Wood's map of 1823 **figure 4**. The lade running south from the Mill Dam was used to power a mill on Bruce Street; hence the name 'Mill Port' for this entrance into the burgh **figure 34**. In the post-medieval period it was recorded that there was a barley mill at the top of Collier Row (Bruce Street) and this seems likely to have been two buildings extending out into the street on Wood's map **figure 4**.[40] The barley mill was removed in 1825 and replaced by a spinning mill.[41] It was recorded in 1892 that a flax-spinning concern had ceased to operate at 'Millport' around 1839.[42] The mill building was marked as the 'Mill Port Factory' on the Ordnance Survey plan surveyed in 1855 and a 'Mill Lead' is shown running past the east side of the building. By the time of the second edition Ordnance Survey surveyed in 1894 the building is still standing but is no longer identified as a factory and the 'Mill Lead' is no longer visible; presumably it had been culverted.

The properties on the east side of Bruce Street occupy a triangular area bordered by Chapel Street to the east. The plots are irregular and do not take the standard form expected for the medieval period. This may have much to do with the location of the mill and associated lade. The only archaeological work undertaken in the vicinity **figure 34** evaluated an area that had been much disturbed in the modern period. A large sandstone culvert running north to south was recorded, although the excavator noted that this did not appear to be in exactly the same position as the 'Mill Lead' marked on the Ordnance Survey plan surveyed in 1855.[43]

As part of the Burgh Survey project an inspection of the cellar beneath no 6 Abbot Street **figure 34**, in former Council Offices that had been built in 1912, revealed a culverted watercourse running east to west. This corresponds well with the line of the 'Tron Burn' shown on Roy's map of 1747–55 **plate 1**.

East end of High Street and East Port

Guildhall Street is a relatively late insertion in the town plan (*see* p 41). Lands on the south side of High Street were purchased in 1758 in order to create the street, which was designed to give access into Abbey Parks.[44] The plots to the east of Guildhall Street and Cross

Wynd Port are generally larger than those to the west and may have been a slightly later development. The single excavation undertaken in this part of town has, however, established that the plots are medieval in origin.[45] Three trenches were excavated within the former premises of the City Bakery before the Kingsgate shopping centre was built **figure 35**. Trenches were placed next to both High Street and Queen Anne Street in order to try to find early frontage buildings and the final trench was located centrally. Near both streets natural clay was encountered directly beneath concrete floors and it would appear that any overlying archaeological deposits had been removed. The trench in the middle of the plot was more productive and confirmed that medieval and post-medieval remains survived. These consisted of post-holes with associated medieval pottery and a lead spindle whorl.[46]

The results from these trenches suggested that the original slope beneath High Street plots was more variable than is now apparent, with later terracing and dumping levelling out the original gradient. The record of a kiln exposed some two metres below the level of High Street at the corner of New Row reinforces this view **figure 35**.[47]

Plots occupied both sides of the road outside the eastern entrance to the town, known as East Port **figure 35**. This was apparent by the time of Roy's survey of 1747–55 **plate 1** and their presence can be traced to medieval times. The plots on the south side of the road that are apparent on the Ordnance Survey plan surveyed in 1855 clearly predate any plots on the east side of New Row. In form the plots outside East Port appear to be medieval in origin and although few in number they are of a comparable width, just over seven metres, to those inside the medieval town. They may have developed between the edge of the burgh and the almshouse (*see* p 25) as an early suburb, although it is as yet uncertain exactly where the almshouse stood, other than that it was in all probability outside the East Port and on the north side of the roadway.

Public buildings and ports

The town's tolbooth had an imposing position at the foot of High Street in the space now occupied by Bridge Street **figure 34** and was present by at least the fifteenth century.[48] The tolbooth that was demolished to make way for Bridge Street in 1769 was of three storeys, and the upper floors were reached by a fan-shaped flight of steps, under which a wide passage connected Kirkgate to Collier Row/Bruce Street **figure 20**.[49]

Following the creation of Bridge Street a replacement building was constructed at the new street's south-eastern corner with High Street.

This building can be seen on the plan by John Wood **figure 4**. The imposing Franco-Scots gothic Category A-listed City Chambers were designed by James Walker and built between 1875 and 1879.[50] They contain a fine bell that bears a date of 1654 and presumably was used as the town bell.

It is thought that the town's medieval tron, the weighing beam in the market, would have been positioned near the tolbooth.[51] Like some other towns in Scotland, Dunfermline did not have an open market place (*see* p 24 and 36). Instead, the length of High Street became a market on allocated days, with booths selling produce at the front of the burgage plots. Different parts of the street would have been dedicated to selling different products. It is as a market that the linear form of High Street, with its crowded frontages and strict divisions of property, is best understood. The location for the pillory is clearly marked on the Ordnance Survey town plan surveyed in 1855 **figure 34**; it was in front of the tolbooth, presumably to ensure maximum public exposure for those being punished (*see* p 24).

The town had a medieval school located in what was once called School Wynd (now Pilmuir Street) at least by the mid fifteenth century **figure 34**.[52] The school had to be rebuilt after the fire of 1624 (*see* p 35) and was again replaced in 1817. It is presumably the latter version that is shown on Wood's plan **figure 4**. Three inscribed stones from the school, one dated to 1625, were built into the Post Office that occupies the site at the time of writing. Two of these inscribed stones remain in fair condition but one appears to be entirely eroded.

Instructions were given that the town was to be surrounded by a ditch on the orders of Edward I in 1303 (*see* p 20); it is not clear whether this replaced any earlier defences. At the least, head dykes located at the end of each burgage plot and maintained by each property owner would have acted as the town's boundary. The recognised routes into the burgh were controlled by five ports (*see* p 19).[53] At the north end of Collier Row/Bruce Street was the Mill Port **figure 34**. The Cross Wynd Port stood at the north end of the street of the same name **figure 34**. The East Port stood at the east end of High Street at the top of New Row **figure 35**, and Rotten Row Port stood somewhere near the foot of Chapel Street **figure 34**. The West Port stood on St Catherine's Wynd **figure 34** and is shown in the far right of **figure 11**. It is unlikely to be coincidental that all these ports appear to have been removed in the second half of the eighteenth century when the burgh began to expand both topographically and financially as a result of the linen trade.[54] The 'Tolbooth Port' seems to have been a gate within the passage underneath the tolbooth stairway,[55] which protruded out into the street, but this did not control access into the burgh.

Religious buildings

A chapel dedicated to St Ninian stood somewhere between High Street and Queen Anne Street/Rotten Row to the east of Collier Row. Its exact position is not now known but it seems logical that it was somewhere in the vicinity of South and North Chapel Streets; these streets are shown on Wood's plan **figure 4** but have been much altered. Wood's map shows a Chapel of Ease at the south end of North Chapel Street. Whether this is related to St Ninian's Chapel is unclear.

In the car park near Chapel Street **figure 34** are two rather incongruous decorative gateways. These are surviving remnants from the Congregational Church, which used to stand on Pilmuir Street.[56]

An almshouse stood outside the East Port possibly on the north side of the street (*see* p 25). There is a large property named Viewfield on the south side of the street marked on Wood's plan **figure 4**. In the medieval period hospitals were commonly referred to as 'Maison Dieu' and elsewhere this may have become corrupted to the name 'Viewfield'.[57] It is possible that here, too, the field known as Viewfield on Wood's map was in some way connected to the almshouse.

Ironworks

Archaeological excavations undertaken in Abbot House revealed that blacksmiths had worked there in the later medieval period.[58] In medieval towns particular industries tended to be concentrated in particular areas and it would seem that Maygate was the centre for iron working until as late as 1815.[59] At that time there was a smithy at the corner of Music Hall Lane and Abbot Street, very close to Abbot House.[60] This was abandoned in 1816, most likely because of problems with access. After this date The Dunfermline Foundry **plate 10**, was established to the north of the town in Clayacres.[61] This venture can be seen on Wood's plan of 1823 **figure 4**. The foundry was the largest in the town throughout the nineteenth century and supplied items as varied as girders for Westminster Palace and pumps for the Nile.[62] The foundry ceased operating in the early 1890s.

A much smaller iron foundry named Grantsbank Foundry was located north of the Dunfermline Foundry **plate 10** and can be seen on the Ordnance Survey town plan surveyed in 1855. No remains relating to Grantsbank Foundry are visible today.

Transy Malleable Iron Works occupied a large site on the south side of Appin Crescent on the north-east outskirts of the town **plate 10**. The company that owned the plant was constituted in 1846 and the layout of this large factory is shown in some detail on the Ordnance Survey plan surveyed in 1855.[63] A note from the *Dunfermline Advertiser* of 11 August 1848 recorded the opening of the works: 'Wednesday, 2 August was a great day … The steam, having been got up in three very large boilers, was set on, and immediately the engine went off in majestic style, playing sweetly and easily in all its parts, and setting in motion those ponderous wheels and beams.'[64] Unfortunately it seems that the venture never lived up to the hopes of the company's shareholders as a pithy description of the works 'as a means, on a large scale, of beating shillings into sixpences' illustrates (sixpences were worth exactly half a shilling).[65] Within a year of 1855 the entire plant was dismantled and destroyed.[66]

The Phoenix Foundry was erected in 1866 on the east side of Phoenix Lane **plate 10**.[67] The works are shown clearly on the Ordnance Survey plan surveyed in 1894 and it appears that the foundry was connected to the Dunfermline/Stirling railway line by a siding equipped with a turntable that must have been designed to allow locomotive engines to access the interior of the main building. Unusually amongst the old foundries of Dunfermline, most of the buildings were still standing at the time of writing.

The textile industry

In the eighteenth century Dunfermline began to grow as the textile and coal-mining industries expanded (*see* pp 48–50). Most of the factories associated with the textile industry were built in the area to the north of High Street.

The Harriebrae Spinning Mill was built just to the south of the confluence of the Baldridge and Castleblair burns **plate 10** and began production in 1817.[68] It is depicted on Wood's map of 1823 **figure 4** and is thought to have ended as a spinning concern about 1852. On the Ordnance Survey plan surveyed in 1855 it was marked as disused and by the time of the survey of 1894 the mill buildings appeared to comprise three separate businesses: a corn mill, a dye works and a damask linen factory. The mills, or at least parts of them, burned down in 1896.[69] Some must have been still standing **figure 29**, or rebuilt, because some remaining buildings were demolished in the early 1970s. Several walls still stand on the site, and early elements of the mill may still survive.

The Knabbie Street Spinning Mill is believed to have been located on the north side of Knabbie Street, now known as Carnegie Drive **plate 10**, and adjacent to what was then the Mill Dam. There are two hand-loom weaving shops depicted in this spot on the Ordnance Survey plan surveyed in 1855. The mill appears to have been founded in 1806 and carried on functioning until 1840.[70] It is not clear who owned the mills when they were surveyed in 1855, but it seems that the site was the location of the Caledonia Linen Works in 1874

29 Harriebrae Mills
(© Crown Copyright:
RCHAMS. Reproduced
courtesy of JR Hume)

and these were destroyed by fire in 1925.[71] No trace of any of these buildings remains.

The Glen Damask Linen Weaving Factory was built in 1840 beside the Tower Burn **plate 10**.[72] It is shown clearly on the Ordnance Survey plan surveyed in 1855 and would appear to have lain underneath the present Glen Bridge. The buildings were still standing when surveyed by the Ordnance Survey in 1894 but they were not marked as a factory at that time and it seems that work had ceased.

Clayacres Spinning Mill occupied a site adjacent to the lade that fed the Mill Dam on the south side of Foundry Street **plate 10**. The Mill begun production around 1827[73] although some buildings appear next to the lade and within the site on Wood's map of 1823 **figure 4**. On the Ordnance Survey plan surveyed in 1855 the complex is shown in some detail and marked as a 'Thread Manufactory'. It seems that this mill survived longer than most in the town and produced flax threads almost to the end of the nineteenth century.[74] There are now no traces left of this complex.

Immediately to the east of Clayacres Mill was the Pilmuir Damask Linen Works of Andrew Reid & Co **plate 10**. Here the first weaving of damask by power loom was tried in 1847, failed, and then resumed with better success in 1849.[75] Showing the experimental nature of this first attempt, the shed was an adjunct to an old hand-loom weaving shop, formerly for 20 looms, marked as warehouse on the first edition Ordnance Survey map, by which time the adjoining power-loom weaving shed was in operation. It is shown on Wood's map as an L-shaped building, and may date from 1816 **figure 4**. A kiln of unique form adjoins to the south of this; iron hooks and bars within it have been interpreted as being for the drying of starched warp threads before that process was superseded by heated rollers (the latter are noted in operation in an account of 1857).[76] The weaving shed roofs show signs of expansion in at least two phases and are lower and shorter in span than those at the later Victoria, Canmore and Castlebrae Works.[77] A row of large brackets between paired columns in the shed show the shafting to have been overhead. The main warehouse has sumptuous first-floor offices and show-rooms, and a great scissor-braced roof over a designing and embroidery floor, completed around 1888–1901.[78] The Italianate frontage on Pilmuir Street was built around 1888-1901.[79] The factory seems to have reached its maximum extent by around 1913 when it had 700 looms.[80] In 1947 the factory was taken over by Dunlop, subsequently Duracord, for the weaving of tyre fabric and this continued until 2005, at which time it was the oldest working weaving shed in Scotland. The buildings are still standing at the time of this Survey, and there are plans to redevelop the site, whilst retaining the more important structures. The Works is Category A-Listed.

Canmore Linen Works **plate 10** was built in 1867[81] and occupied the site previously taken up by the Mill Dam.[82] This large factory was owned by J & J Alexander and employed 800 people. In 1932 a Swiss company, Winterthur, that produced silk material, bought the building and converted the factory to this end. The building closed in 1970 but still stands, divided into Thomson's 'World of Furniture' and several smaller units, at the time of writing. The design is attributed to the millwrights and engineers Robertson and Orchar, who are known to have built factories in Dunfermline besides their similar jute and linen weaving sheds in Dundee, Forfar, Kirriemuir, Brechin, Perth, and Freuchie.[83] Looms and finishing machinery were also likely to have been supplied by the same firm. Canmore seems to have been the first by Robertson and Orchar in the town and as it established a pattern for the others it will be described here. The main weaving shed comprises broad-span north-lit roofs (so as to avoid direct light) of timber trusses spanning between cast-iron columns. Because columns could be more than ten metres apart the line shafting was in most cases placed in tunnels below the floor and so represents some archaeological potential (line shafting and bevel gearing was found *in situ* at Seafield Works, Dundee, also by Robertson and Orchar, for example). Depending on the lie of the land, a two-storey warehouse might be built in such a way that its ground floor extends beneath that of the main factory (as also at St Margaret's Works for example, once it had expanded in 1893).

Set perpendicular to the weaving shed is the engine house, marked by characteristic tall arched windows. The early engines were of the

30 Victoria Works chimney, boiler house and beam engine house (courtesy of Mark Watson)

beam type: the cross entablature on which the beam rocked survives at Victoria Works (1876) **figure 30**. Horizontal engines could occupy less room and are likely to have been favoured at Canmore. The largest works found it necessary to supplement power, and did so by installing vertical engines: the cluster of engine houses by the chimney of Pilmuir Works is evidence of this. The ashlar foundations showing the layout, flywheel pit and separate condenser, will usually survive and offer potential for archaeological analysis. Next door at Canmore Works are three lower arched openings that each fronted a Lancashire boiler.

The warehouse is a distinctive element of the damask factories, partly as advertisements for linen merchants, but also for the many support functions needed for the design of table cloths, cutting of Jacquard pattern cards, checking sewing and embroidering the cloth, for which a broad unencumbered space was needed at the top floor: large examples are at St Leonard's, Pilmuir and St Margaret's Works, smaller ones at Albany and Victoria Works, which would indicate that the checking and sewing took place there within the overall shed.

Castleblair Damask Linen Works was opened on the east side of Mill Street in 1868 **plate 10**. Like the Canmore Works it was bought by a Swiss company to manufacture silk fabric. The silk manufacturing ran from 1925 until 1967[84] when it became a clothing factory, Castleblair Ltd, which supplied Marks & Spencer. Some of the buildings were still standing at the time of writing.

St Margaret's Damask Linen Works was originally located on the north side of Foundry Street **plate 10** and eventually expanded to occupy the ground occupied by the Dunfermline Foundry. The Works opened in 1870[85] and is shown clearly on the Ordnance Survey plan surveyed in 1894. The factory closed in 1982 and the main weaving shed buildings were demolished in 1984.[86] Some buildings, the earliest dated to 1900, still survive and are Category B-listed.

The Caledonia Damask Linen Works stood on the north side of Carnegie Drive **plate 10**, over what had been the Knabbie Street Works (*see* p 87). The Caledonia Works was established in 1874[87] and the building can be seen on the Ordnance Survey plan surveyed in 1894.[88] The entire factory was destroyed by fire in 1925 and the buildings subsequently demolished; there is now no trace of the former works and the site is occupied by a fire station.[89]

The Albany Damask Linen Works was located toward the west end of Gardeners Street **plate 10** and opened in 1874.[90] The Ordnance Survey town plan surveyed in 1894 shows the buildings as they were then. The factory closed in 1936 but re-opened the next year for the manufacture of silk and artificial silk fabrics.[91] This ceased in 1957 and a large part of the buildings were destroyed by fire in 1974.[92] Some of the factory buildings still survive, fronting onto Gardeners Street and listed as Category 'C' (S).[93]

The Victoria Damask Linen Works was built in 1876 on the east side of Pilmuir Street **plate 10**.[94] The mill was powered by steam and can be seen on the Ordnance Survey plan surveyed in 1894. The works were closed in 1926 for linen production but bought to produce embroidery in 1928. Later they began to manufacture clothes and finally closed in 2005. The buildings are largely intact at the time of writing and Category B-listed, but redevelopment of the factory site is proposed. Most of the structures date from the later nineteenth century and the beam engine house is the most complete of its type in Dunfermline.[95]

Post-medieval buildings

High Street contains some vernacular buildings dating to the eighteenth century and fine commercial buildings from the nineteenth century **figures 7 and 8**. Modern developments such as the Kingsgate shopping centre have swept away a fair number of historic buildings but many still survive and can be readily picked out along the length of the street.[96]

Buildings from the post-medieval period can have a complicated history of development that results in a complex amalgamation of structures. Such an example was visited at no 19 Bruce Street **figure 34** as part of the Survey. Here redevelopment had exposed old stone and brickwork behind more modern coverings. It was apparent that many individual buildings and phases of use could be discerned. In *Viagraphia Dunfermlynensis* Henderson states that the property was somewhat complex – having a low wall with railing behind and buildings in the shape of the letter 'L'. They served a number of purposes: in one part the first bank in Dunfermline was established (Bank of Scotland); there was a dye mill, the wheel of which was activated by a large dog running inside it; purchased by R & J Kerr, table linen manufacturers, in 1823 a small two-storey house was added to serve as 'the commercial bank'.[97] The entire property was sold to William Kinnis in 1849, hence the name it acquired of Kinnis Court. Remnants of a Damask Linen Warehouse depicted on the Ordnance Survey plan surveyed in 1855 may still be seen, as are the numerous stages of stairways as access was given to sections of the property as they descended down the bank of the Tower Burn. The recording of such buildings often reveals a complicated history that sheds light on the development of the town as a whole.

Sited as they are on the sloping side of Tower Burn, the properties along the west side of Kirkgate and Bruce Street all appear to have cellars. Some of these were observed during research and it was noted that the cellar at no 1 Bruce Street had once been fitted with bins for the storage of grain. These were probably fed from pavement level by chutes that are still in place. Perhaps these premises functioned as a grocery or a bakery at one point in the past.

Building alterations at no 24 Bruce Street in 1996 revealed vaulted drying kilns, flagstone floors, a staircase leading to an upper level and a flagstone courtyard. A stone wall running parallel to Bruce Street displayed a carved stone near to the lintel of a grilled window. The Ordnance Survey map in 1855 indicates the building was a calender works. A little further up the street at nos 28–34 Bruce Street is an interesting old building (Category C(S)-listed), now in a poor state of repair. Its nineteenth-century appearance may belie an earlier structure.

In 1996 during a programme of refurbishment of buildings in Maygate, no 32 had cement cladding removed, which revealed two stone arches at ground level **figure 25**. It was assumed that these originally functioned as an enclosed walkway or arcade on the ground floor, as may be witnessed in many burghs, with a wooden building above. The wooden building was presumably replaced with a stone structure, possibly following the 1624 fire (*see* pp 35–6). Interestingly, alterations to the rooms on the west side of the ground floor revealed that the joists were raw, trimmed tree trunks. These could have come from the Garvock estate, denuded of trees as a result of the rebuilding process post-fire (*see* pp 35–6). This is a fine example of what may be hidden behind later façades, as is a large stone arch seen within the premises occupying no 4 Maygate **figure 23**.[98] This would once have been an entrance, big enough for a horse and cart, into a yard to the rear of a frontage building.

Further east, at the corner of Canmore Street and St Margaret Street – no 1 Canmore Street, once the St Margaret's Hotel and presently called Urban Grill, is Category C(S)-listed. It is probably what lies underground here that is of greater interest. The northern wall of the building's cellar is likely to incorporate a stretch of abbey precinct wall and a post-medieval doorway through this gives access to a covered passageway that runs around the outside of the building below street level. The northern part of this underground passage gives a good impression of what 'In Between the Wa's' must have been like during the medieval period (*see* p 18) and includes an intact small well still full of clear water and probably fed from an underground spring. At right angles, the passageway runs in a southerly direction and ends in a blocked culvert, which may have been part of the drainage system of the abbey precinct. The passageway may have been created to ensure the cellar remained dry. It also illustrates that the medieval ground surface here was well below that of present-day Canmore Street. This means archaeological survival should be excellent. Importantly, much of the abbey's precinct wall may be surviving elsewhere in Canmore Street.

These are merely a small sample of the many listed buildings throughout the town. Further information on others of significance may be found in the Dunfermline Burgh Statutory List.

Area 3: New Row and Netherton

New Row occupies a north to south slope and the properties lining it were presumably developed when the medieval town outgrew its limits, although it seems likely that the route was created much earlier to provide access between Netherton and the upper town (*see* p 18). Modern development has swept away most of the street's historic buildings but it has hosted an important excavation as a result. Netherton sits at the foot of a slope below the abbey precinct and was also an early settlement. It has seen a significant amount of modern development and consequently has lost most of its medieval character **figure 19**.

Burgage plots in New Row and Netherton

The development along New Row lay outside the East Port and seems to have been outside the burgh defences. It was the location for an extremely informative excavation in 1993 that confirmed the archaeological potential of the town **figure 35**.[99] The earliest deposits suggested that the area was cultivated after the precinct of the abbey was established but before being divided into burgage plots in the late fifteenth century.[100] The plots seem to have been broader than those

on High Street with widths up to ten metres.[101] The excavation
uncovered a corn-drying kiln located to the rear of a medieval plot.[102]
There was also evidence of the burgh's conversion into a linen
production centre in the post-medieval period with the recording
of a loom stance.

The excavation confirmed that New Row was a late-medieval
development along a pre-existing route running from Netherton to
East Port. From the appearance of Roy's plan **plate 1** the west side
may have been more developed than the east, and it seems that the
ground occupied by Comely Park House (Category C(S)-listed)
figure 35 was open gardens until at least the eighteenth century.

Netherton was recorded as early as the fourteenth century (*see*
p 18). The medieval plots ran off a single, east to west street, and
are clearly shown on Roy's plan **plate 1**. The street plan visible today
has been much altered with Moodie Street developed between the
time of Roy's plan in the mid eighteenth century and Wood's in
1823 **plate 1 and figure 4**. Elgin Street was inserted after 1823, and
may have obliterated any signs of St Mary's Chapel, but the line
is shown by Wood as an intended development. More recent
modern developments on both sides of the street have removed
most recognisable medieval properties. Many medieval plots could
still be seen on the Ordnance Survey plan surveyed in 1855, and their
width appears to have been closer to those in High Street (around six
or seven metres) than those in New Row. This observation offers
some confirmation that Netherton was an early development.

Lady's Mill

Lady's Mill lay at the west end of Netherton, on the west side of
Tower Burn as shown by Wood in 1823 **figure 4**. A bridge had been
built by the time the area was recorded by Wood. This was not
apparent on the plan made by Roy in 1747–55 **plate 1** but a bridge
was historically recorded at the end of Netherton in 1649 (*see* p 36).
The mill was recorded in the medieval period and presumably would
have been driven by a wheel.

A building named Lady's Mill **plate 10** still stands nearby but it
is not on the same site as that shown on Wood's plan. The building
named Lady's Mill today is shown on the Ordnance Survey plan
surveyed in 1894 as a sawmill and turning works.

A disparity in the line of watercourses shown in the vicinity of the
mill on the Wood and Roy plans **figure 4 and plate 1** may be of interest.
Roy appears to show a lade being diverted from the Tower Burn,
perhaps for use at Lady's Mill, then discharging back into the Tower
Burn. Wood, however, shows only one channel[103] and this appears to
follow the line of the possible lade shown by Roy. It is possible that

other alterations to the watercourse a little to the south were being undertaken at this time.

Roy's map also appears to show a watercourse at the east end of Netherton **plate 1**. It would appear that this watercourse originated at the Mill Dam, ran through the town and abbey precinct, ran past the end of Netherton before continuing south to meet the Lyne Burn. Roy depicts some buildings to the east of this watercourse's confluence with the Lyne Burn. These do not appear to be beside the road to Queensferry and are not consistent with the known location of St Leonard's Hospital (*see* p 25). It is worth noting that these buildings could be medieval in origin and possibly, given their location, another mill.

Religious buildings

St Leonard's Chapel and Hospital **plate 10** are thought to have been medieval foundations (*see* p 25) although they were not documented until after the Reformation.[104] The site's location was marked on the Ordnance Survey town plan surveyed in 1855 and at that time the graveyard associated with it was respected by the surrounding St Leonard's Factory. It was noted that many bones were exposed in 1890, and this implies that the graveyard was disturbed at that time.[105] Some 40 skeletons were excavated in the graveyard in 1975, although there is only a short notice describing this work.[106]

There was a chapel dedicated to St Mary at the west end of Netherton opposite Moodie Street **figure 19**. The last traces of it were removed in 1814 and presumably Elgin Street now overlies the site.[107]

Perdieus Mount

To the south of Netherton and near the confluence of the Lyne and Tower Burns is the Scheduled Ancient Monument named Perdieus Mount **plate 10**. This was recorded by RCAHMS in 1933 as a large earthen mound in a low-lying field, with a height of around four and a half metres.[108] The Mount was classified as a possible motte hill at that time, but when visited by the Ordnance Survey in 1974 it was noted that this classification could not be confirmed because the monument was 'too mutilated'.[109] An archaeological watching brief was undertaken on the excavation of foundation and service trenches on a house adjacent to the monument in 1995.[110] These extended to a depth of half a metre and the monitoring archaeologist noted that the lower deposit in the trenches appeared to be some kind of hillwash. Hillwash is a term archaeologists use to describe deposits that accumulate at the base of slopes as a result of soil movement.

It can frequently cover and protect earlier archaeological remains. Unfortunately, and perhaps because of the covering hillwash, nothing was exposed that could clarify the nature of the Mount.

The name of the monument may suggest that it is not a motte. It has been suggested that 'Perdieus' is derived from the Old Irish word 'Pardus', which referred to a religious garden.[111] Other place-name evidence suggests that there may have been a religious establishment in the vicinity of Dunfermline before the documented marriage of Malcolm and Margaret.[112]

It is worth pointing out in relation to this monument that the course of the Tower Burn as it ran south from Lady's Mill to the Lyne Burn seems to have been altered in relatively recent times. As depicted on Roy's map of 1747–55 **plate 1**, the main course of the stream seems to have been further west. Another recently discovered plan made in 1766 **plate 3** shows the course of the stream clearly to the west of the monument, which is shown as a tree-covered mound.[113] Between 1766 and the survey of Wood in 1823 **figure 4** the line of the stream seems to have been entirely diverted into a canalised course to the east of the Mount. Originally the Mount would have been located strategically between the Lyne and Tower Burns (at one point referred to as the 'Ferm') and it is perhaps a contender for the 'Dun' from which Dunfermline may be derived (*see* pp 3 and 15), although there are problems with this interpretation of the place-name.[114] Current flood-prevention scheme works being undertaken by Fife Council may have an effect on the Mount as the burn flows close by.

Industry in Netherton

Foregate Foundry was located at the junction of New Row and Netherton Broad Street **plate 10**. It was a short-lived venture lasting from the early 1820s until 1840.[115] After 1840 the works were converted for damask-weaving hand-looms and then from 1849 to 1857 it was used for the weaving of 'homlier' fabrics.[116] The *Dunfermline Press* of 1892[117] contains a related story that paints a vivid picture of this part of town when the foundry was operating. Apparently the foundry was the second of two obstacles that horse riders had to negotiate on this route into town. First they had to pass the Spittal Smithy, a little to the south-east of the town, where an enterprising smith had erected a windmill designed to swing his hammer. The windmill was said to have a 'most uncouth and frightful appearance' when turning and was apt to spook horses. They then had to run the gamut of the foundry's noisy furnaces. Apparently this led to several accidents and arguments that ceased only when the foundry went out of business and the smith decided his windmill was of no great benefit. The position where the foundry once stood is now hidden beneath the roadway and roundabout at the junction of St Margaret's Drive, Bothwell Street and Netherton Broad Street.

A spinning mill was constructed at Brucefield in 1792 **plate 10** and it has wrongly[118] been claimed that this was only the second of its type in Scotland.[119] There seems to have been some confusion over whether the mill was water or steam powered.[120] The mill was also the location of an evening school. An accidental fire broke out in 1825 and caused enough damage to bring an end to flax spinning.[121] After the fire the buildings were used for yarn bleaching until 1845. Following this the mill fell into disrepair and in 1850 it was dismantled to provide building material for the Music Hall.[122] Old Mill Court now occupies the site of the mill.

Milton Green Spinning Mill **plate 10** was opened around 1826 and functioned until around 1840.[123] The mill continued to have a useful function after this as it was 'made the happy haunt of all sorts of preachers, orators, fiddlers, and dancers'.[124] It was marked as ruinous on the Ordnance Survey town plan surveyed in 1855.

The Bothwell Damask Linen Works was located on the east side of Elgin Street to the rear of the Netherton Broad Street frontage **plate 10**. It was opened in 1865[125] and is first shown on the Ordnance Survey plan surveyed in 1894. The factory closed in 1932 and was demolished in the 1950s, although the former office building, Bothwell House, still survives.[126]

The St Leonard's Damask Linen Works **figure 10a** was founded on the site of the medieval hospital (*see* p 25) in 1851.[127] The factory was extended in 1860 and 1883 to become the largest linen works in the town. It was perhaps the most important factory in Dunfermline and in 1913 when production was at its peak there were1,000 looms operating.[128] The factory closed in 1989 and an Asda superstore now occupies much of the site. The Category B-listed office and warehouse buildings had already been converted to flats in 1983 and still survive.

The railway bridge and ashlar-lined culvert built in 1832 at no 10 Forth Street to allow access for the Elgin Railway, which can be seen on the first edition Ordnance Survey map, is Category C(S)-listed.[129] This is about to be demolished as part of Fife Council's flood-prevention scheme. The gateposts of the railway level crossing may still be seen at no 12 Forth Street and also on the west side on the erstwhile crossing.

31 Old view of the Rhodes
(from D Thomson)

32 The Rhodes, 2007
(courtesy of Bert
McEwan)

Post-medieval development

The area between Netherton and the south boundary of the former abbey precinct was developed some time between Roy's map of 1747–55 and Wood's map of 1823 **plate 1 and figure 4**. A marriage lintel incorporated into a building at no 31 Rolland Street **figure 35** provides a more specific date of 1794.

A little to the south-east of Netherton is an impressive dwelling known as The Rhodes, **figures 31 and 32** which has been claimed as 'The Oldest Inhabited House in Dunfermline'.[130] It bears a date-stone inscribed with initials and 1695. It is harled white and T-shaped in plan with a crow-stepped gable.[131]

The area to the east of New Row, known as Comely Park, was laid out in 1875.[132] Perhaps the most imposing building in this attractive suburb is Comely Park House **figure 35**, a Category C(S)-listed structure. Although remodelled a little after 1875 the house incorporates an earlier structure of 1785.[133] A Category B-listed sundial, dated to 1786, is in the garden[134] but may have been moved from elsewhere.[135]

Area 4: the abbey precinct

The impressive buildings and architecture of the abbey have been discussed in detail elsewhere, and a full description will not be attempted here.[136] This section will focus on archaeological work that has been undertaken within the precinct and what we know of its organisation.

The church and surviving buildings

In 1916 excavations within the Abbey Church **figure 34** uncovered stone foundations that are generally accepted as belonging to the church founded by Queen Margaret in the eleventh century.[137] It seems to have been a simple and small building with a length of around 26 metres. Inside there were several burials, possibly of members from the royal family.[138] The church was rebuilt as a much larger and more elaborate structure when David I made it an abbey around 1128.[139] The relics of St Margaret were transferred to a chapel built for the purpose at the east end of the church in 1250.[140]

In addition to the church itself some other monastic buildings survive, notably the fourteenth-century refectory **figure 34** built by King Robert Bruce following the supposed destruction of the monastery by Edward I.[141] The gatehouse **figure 34** positioned at the south-west corner of the refectory was confirmed to be a later structure by excavations in 1975.[142] On the other side of Monastery Street the kitchens and guest-house/palace (Scheduled Ancient Monument and Category A-listed) **figure 34 and plate 4** survive. These buildings would have been the most substantial in the monastery complex and this probably explains their survival.

The cloister would have been to the south of the church and the standing refectory still defines its south side.[143] From the refectory the standing remains extend further east, through what used to be the monks' reredorter (or latrine). The monastery would have had an advanced water-management system and a substantial lade, now silted up but clearly visible, can be seen emerging from the north wall of the latrine. This would originally have carried away sewage and possibly fed into another lade to the south-east that fed the Heugh Mills, as shown on a plan made in 1865.[144] The wall that the lade emerges from can be traced further east, beside the War Memorial **figure 34** where it functions as a retaining wall for the graveyard and is dotted with narrow weep-holes designed for drainage. This stretch of wall is later and seems likely to date to the post-medieval period and during a visit as part of the Survey a fragment of fifteenth- or sixteenth-century pottery was retrieved from some spoil (presumably created by a small mammal) at the entrance to one of the weep-holes.

In addition to the surviving buildings, there would have been many others in the precinct, and archaeological excavations have helped identify several.

The precinct wall and buried buildings

The precinct wall would appear to still have been standing, at least in the main, at the time of Roy's survey in 1747–55 **plate 1**. It followed a northern line along Maygate and Canmore Street and part of the wall still stands as a Scheduled Ancient Monument on Canmore Street **figure 35**. The eastern line ran to the rear of the western New Row properties. Excavations around the precinct wall on both the northern and eastern boundaries have confirmed this line and a medieval date.[145] Also, a building assessment of a passageway that survives around the cellar of the building, at the corner of Canmore Street and St Margaret Street, once the St Margaret's Hotel **figure 34** suggested that, although probably post-medieval in date, parts of the standing building might include elements of the medieval precinct wall.[146] The excavations at New Row **figure 35** suggested that here the precinct wall had been predated by a ditch, which had functioned as a simple boundary up until the fourteenth or fifteenth century, when it had been filled and covered by a pathway.[147]

Interestingly, the course of the ditch at New Row was not necessarily identical to that of the later wall, and it might have veered westward while the wall continued to the south. An earlier southern extent of the precinct may have been preserved in the line of modern Buchanan Street. Another interesting observation from the New Row excavation was that the ditch may have acted as an open drain, or even originated as a watercourse.[148] As discussed earlier, it may be the case that a watercourse is depicted on Roy's map **plate 1** in the vicinity of the precinct wall here.

At Abbot House it could not be established what the earliest boundary had been, wall or ditch, but it was clear that a wall was present here by the fourteenth century, and so earlier than at New Row.[149] Perhaps the earlier construction of a precinct wall at Abbot House reflected the higher status of this part of the abbey, with more importance attached to constructing an impressive boundary near to the church and shrine of St Margaret. Both excavations established that a flagstone pathway ran inside the precinct wall, and this may have carried on round the entire circuit.

The southern and western parts of the precinct boundary are not so well understood. The standing structure called the Nether Yett **plate 6** is believed to mark a gateway into the precinct **figure 34** and for this reason it is generally thought the southern boundary of the precinct ran along Priory Lane, although as already noted the

New Row excavations suggested that an earlier ditched boundary may have existed further north (*see* p 100). On an engraving by John Slezer in the late seventeenth century **figure 17**, the wall turned northward from the Nether Yett before turning west along the line of Monastery Street to meet the east side of the refectory or reredorter.[150] However, it is not clear if this is an accurate depiction.

The Heugh Mills were presumably part of the abbey complex and they lie outside the line depicted by Slezer. Similarly, this line would not have included the palace/guest-house, which was an integral part of the abbey. It has been suggested that the precinct wall may have split at the Nether Yett with one branch running west while another headed to the north before turning at Monastery Street.[151] The area between these two lines seems to have been a distinct location known as St Lawrence's Yard.[152] A wall marked as Palace Wall on the Ordnance Survey town plan surveyed in 1855 follows the line running directly west from the Nether Yett and perhaps originated as the medieval precinct wall **figure 34**. Certainly the north face of the Nether Yett is smooth, suggesting that the precinct wall did not carry on in this direction, as this would have left a scar on the surviving face.

This small piece of physical evidence seems to support the suggestion that the precinct wall carried on to the west from the Nether Yett. The line of the Palace Wall, as shown on the Ordnance Survey plan, can still be followed through Pittencrieff Park and many parts of it are still defined by a standing wall that is comparable to the identified stretches of precinct wall in Canmore Street. This view is supported by the Historic Scotland Statutory List information for the former Abbey Church Manse at no 1 Moodie Street, which states that the wall to the north of this property's garden was the boundary for the abbey.[153]

On the west side of the precinct it has been suggested that the chapel and almshouse of St Catherine **figure 34** may have been within the abbey precinct and perhaps represent a successor to the monastic almonry.[154] The remains of the chapel **figure 16** are a Scheduled Ancient Monument and might be well preserved, if there were not trees growing out of the upper structure, which is likely to destabilise the building. Although they are somewhat hidden from the street, because of a difference in ground level and a covering of vegetation, the walls still stand to a height of around two metres.

Anne of Denmark built her residence over the north Palace Yard Gatehouse when she inherited the abbey lands **figures 11 and 34** [155] A fine perspective view of this residence is given on a manuscript map drawn in 1766 **plate 3**.[156] Presumably the Palace Yard Gatehouse prevented access to restricted areas of the precinct. Another gatehouse, now known as the Pends (Scheduled Ancient Monument and Category

33 Archaeological excavations at Abbot House in 1988–94 (courtesy of Abbot House)

A-listed) **figure 34** survives further south and may have provided access between the kitchen on the south side of Monastery Street and the refectory.[157]

The earliest remains encountered during the Abbot House excavations **figure 33** suggested that the northern part of the precinct was the location of stone-built workshops.[158] These were constructed as early as the twelfth century and were associated with metalworking.[159] Later, in the fourteenth to fifteenth centuries this area was converted for use as a cemetery **figure 33**. This kind of systematic reorganisation of space within the precinct was also recognised during the New Row excavations.

Undoubtedly, the most impressive building in the outer precinct is Abbot House **figures 14 and 15**. The archaeological investigations within the surviving structure suggested it was constructed in the mid to late fifteenth century and so the popular supposition that it had been the abbot's residence at one time could be accurate.[160] The front wall of the house was tied into the precinct wall and fronted onto Maygate. It would have been one of very few stone-built houses in the burgh and, perhaps surprisingly, the ground floor was used for smithing at some point during the late medieval period.

Elsewhere in the precinct, excavation has returned intriguing results. Trial trenching to the south of Carnegie Library **figure 34** encountered a lade running through the middle of the site.[161] The lade was predated by an open watercourse, which had been filled with midden including preserved organic artefacts. Intriguingly, some wall foundations were uncovered at a depth of 1.4 metres below the current ground surface. These were unfortunately not dated but seem likely to be medieval.[162]

On the east side of St Margaret Street, and opposite the Library, **figure 34** a fairly large open area was excavated in 2004.[163] This revealed a part of the precinct that had been prone to flooding given the eight or so culverts discovered (*see* p 37), and which had been used for cultivation throughout the medieval period. The orientation of the culverts had been altered at one time, and this may reflect one of the reorganisations of the precinct that were evident at Abbot House and New Row.[164] Interestingly, the earliest culverts revealed during excavation on the east side of St Margaret Street **figure 34** all drained water away from the abbey. The east side of St Margaret Street would appear to have been close to, and immediately west of, a square feature fed and drained by a stream or lade depicted on Roy's map **plate 1**. It is tempting to link this feature with references to a fishpond in this part of the precinct (*see* p 37). There are seventeenth-century references to this pond overflowing, which caused flooding in the graveyard to the north of the abbey.[165] Drainage would also have been a problem that the monks would have faced and the culverts revealed on the east side of St Margaret Street seem likely to have been designed as a solution. Presumably they worked by carrying water south and east away from the centre of the precinct.

It is also interesting that the line followed by St Margaret Street appears to mark such a dramatic change in the archaeological remains, with cultivation on the east side and structures to the west, beneath the Library car park. This suggests that St Margaret Street followed the line of an earlier medieval boundary. A corresponding line is shown on Roy's map between the pond and the core of the precinct **plate 1**, which supports this suggestion.

At no 76 St Margaret Street **figure 34** an evaluation and watching brief were carried out in 2000–01.[166] Although this work was limited, it did encounter a substantial clay-bonded wall running north to south. The excavator suggested that the build and substantial nature of the wall could be compatible with that of the precinct wall.[167] This wall is not on a line that has been closely associated with that of the precinct boundary, but there is a chance that a 'kink' in the south-west corner of the precinct wall did extend this far north along St Margaret Street, as it appears to on Slezer's view.[168] Frustratingly, given the context of possible early settlement at

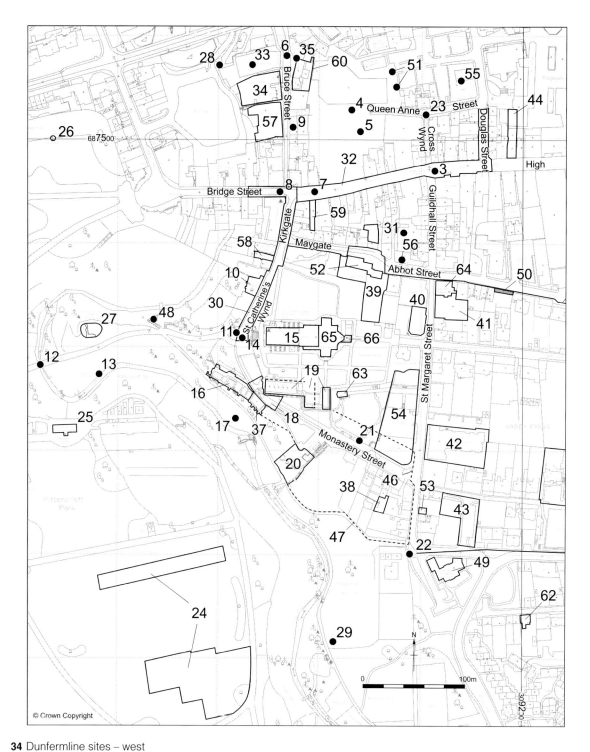

34 Dunfermline sites – west

(Reproduced by permission of Ordnance Survey on behalf of HMSO © Crown Copyright 2007.
All rights reserved. Ordnance Survey Licence number 100013329)

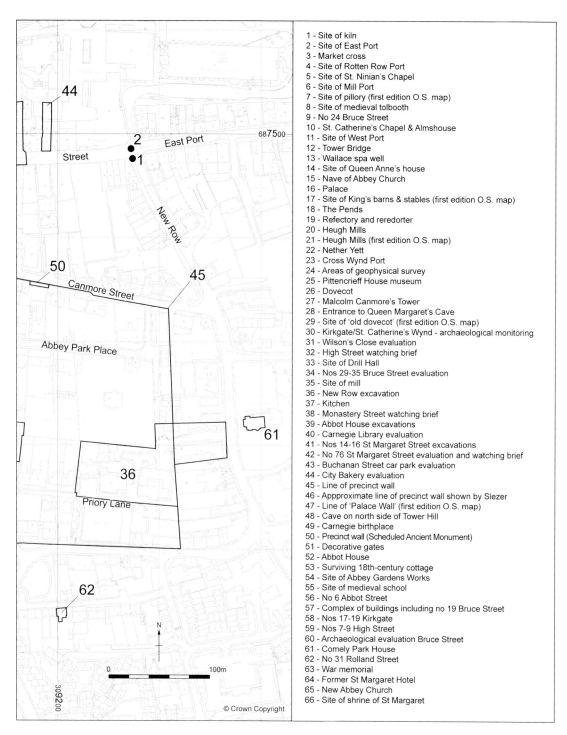

1 - Site of kiln
2 - Site of East Port
3 - Market cross
4 - Site of Rotten Row Port
5 - Site of St. Ninian's Chapel
6 - Site of Mill Port
7 - Site of pillory (first edition O.S. map)
8 - Site of medieval tolbooth
9 - No 24 Bruce Street
10 - St. Catherine's Chapel & Almshouse
11 - Site of West Port
12 - Tower Bridge
13 - Wallace spa well
14 - Site of Queen Anne's house
15 - Nave of Abbey Church
16 - Palace
17 - Site of King's barns & stables (first edition O.S. map)
18 - The Pends
19 - Refectory and reredorter
20 - Heugh Mills
21 - Heugh Mills (first edition O.S. map)
22 - Nether Yett
23 - Cross Wynd Port
24 - Areas of geophysical survey
25 - Pittencrieff House museum
26 - Dovecot
27 - Malcolm Canmore's Tower
28 - Entrance to Queen Margaret's Cave
29 - Site of 'old dovecot' (first edition O.S. map)
30 - Kirkgate/St. Catherine's Wynd - archaeological monitoring
31 - Wilson's Close evaluation
32 - High Street watching brief
33 - Site of Drill Hall
34 - Nos 29-35 Bruce Street evaluation
35 - Site of mill
36 - New Row excavation
37 - Kitchen
38 - Monastery Street watching brief
39 - Abbot House excavations
40 - Carnegie Library evaluation
41 - Nos 14-16 St Margaret Street excavations
42 - No 76 St Margaret Street evaluation and watching brief
43 - Buchanan Street car park evaluation
44 - City Bakery evaluation
45 - Line of precinct wall
46 - Appproximate line of precinct wall shown by Slezer
47 - Line of 'Palace Wall' (first edition O.S. map)
48 - Cave on north side of Tower Hill
49 - Carnegie birthplace
50 - Precinct wall (Scheduled Ancient Monument)
51 - Decorative gates
52 - Abbot House
53 - Surviving 18th-century cottage
54 - Site of Abbey Gardens Works
55 - Site of medieval school
56 - No 6 Abbot Street
57 - Complex of buildings including no 19 Bruce Street
58 - Nos 17-19 Kirkgate
59 - Nos 7-9 High Street
60 - Archaeological evaluation Bruce Street
61 - Comely Park House
62 - No 31 Rolland Street
63 - War memorial
64 - Former St Margaret Hotel
65 - New Abbey Church
66 - Site of shrine of St Margaret

35 Dunfermline sites – east

(Reproduced by permission of Ordnance Survey on behalf of HMSO © Crown Copyright 2007.
All rights reserved. Ordnance Survey Licence number 100013329)

Dunfermline, a ditch that ran beneath the wall on a north-east to south-west alignment, did not produce any material that could suggest a date.[169]

A watching brief to the rear of Monastery Street buildings **figure 34** recorded a culvert on a north-east to south-west alignment. This work confirmed that deep deposits in this area are likely to have protected any early remains.[170] It should also be noted that in the garden of no 1 Monastery Street (also using the garden of no 3), currently owned by Carnegie Dunfermline Trust, there are several stones and slates which may have their origins from the abbey complex. If development here is considered, these are of potential archaeological interest.

An evaluation beneath a current car park between Buchanan Street and Priory Lane was carried out in 1996–7 **figure 34**.[171] This work established that the area must have lain within the abbey precinct and it was the location for substantial buildings, perhaps supplied with water by a large culvert.

The precinct in the post-medieval period

The Reformation had a dramatic effect on the abbey and by 1563 the buildings were dilapidated and hazardous.[172] The church did remain a place of worship for the townspeople, who might have been relieved when the abbey was granted to Anne of Denmark in 1589. Anne built a residence on the west side of the church **figure 11**.[173] On her husband's accession to the English throne in 1603 the palace became more peripheral to the royal couple, although it was used again in the reign of Charles I.[174]

The later seventeenth and eighteenth centuries saw much decay of the abbey buildings (*see* pp 29–30) and it was not until the nineteenth century that remedial work was undertaken and the old abbey church was converted into the building we see today.[175] The churchyard continued in use throughout this period and contains a rich variety of sandstone monuments. Many recumbent examples will be hidden beneath the surface, as confirmed by an archaeological watching brief during installation of the lighting system around the church in 1993.[176]

The growing post-medieval town encroached on the former precinct in the eighteenth and nineteenth centuries. As noted in Chapter 3, the Abbey Park was given over to bleaching in 1731 and canals were dug to facilitate this process. It is possible that the possible watercourse and pond shown on Roy's plan **plate 1** were used as part of the bleaching process. This venture was in decline by the later eighteenth century and a recently discovered plan made in 1865 shows all water being directed to the south to emerge at Heugh Mills.[177] When Pennant visited the town in the 1770s, he implied the watercourse was flagged and ran down to Heugh Mills.

After the bleachfield went out of use Abbey Parks became a desirable place to live and the area is full of fine villas with private gardens. Some smaller and simpler dwellings survive further to the south toward the bottom of St Margaret Street, such as the Carnegie birthplace (Category B-listed) **figure 34**. At the time of writing a little cottage survives at no 92 St Margaret Street **figure 34 and plate 7**; it is simple, unpretentious and likely to be eighteenth-century in date. It seems to have been built using stone robbed from the abbey complex.

The former precinct did not see much industrial development but there were some exceptions. The largest factory in the former precinct was the Abbey Gardens Damask Linen Works **figure 34**. This was opened in 1860 on the west side of St Margaret Street and extended north from Monastery Street.[178] The buildings are clearly shown on the Ordnance Survey plan surveyed in 1855 and were expanded in 1866.[179] The works closed in 1928.[180] Wood's map of 1823 **figure 4** shows a number of buildings on the same site. These are not labelled and it has been suggested that a brewer occupied the site.[181]. The area is now occupied by car parks and gardens, although a standing wall forming the north boundary of the site retains features such as a fireplace and was probably part of the linen works.

Remains relating to Heugh Mills, a Scheduled Ancient Monument, survive to the south of the claustral range **figure 34 and plate 5**. These were powered using water wheels that ran off 'The Lead', which can still be seen, as can the marks the wheels scored out of the sandstone walls. According to Pennant, writing in the 1770s there were five mills, three for corn, one for flax and one for beating iron.[182] Slezer's engraving of the late seventeenth century **figure 17** shows only two mills on 'The Lead', but also includes two kilns further west.[183] On a painting of 1793, discussed in an article of 1966, there appear to be three mills, possibly for grinding corn, and the water wheels of two are shown.[184] The lade was carried over the wheels in wooden channels and linen was spread out to dry or bleach to the east.[185] The painting also shows a large octagonal kiln for drying grain to the west of the mills.

At the time the article on the mills was written, in 1966, the surviving walls of the buildings were standing to a height of up to 20 feet (just over 6 metres) and the author noted that there were at least two different types of masonry evident. At the time of writing this Survey, some 40 years later, there are still at least two types of masonry present but the remains survive to only half the height noted in 1966.[186]

The Ordnance Survey town plan surveyed in 1855 shows another Heugh Mill, noted as producing flour, using the same lade further upslope on the other side of Monastery Street **figure 34**. The same map also shows a site marked as 'King's barns and stables' to the south of the palace **figure 34**. It was noted when visited by the Ordnance Survey in 1974 that this was an unlikely situation for these buildings.[187] There may have been some ruined buildings here that had been misidentified but, if so, no trace of them survived in 1974.

Notes

1 Perry, 'Dunfermline', 787.
2 SUAT, Archive Report of Excavations at Malcolm Canmore's Tower 1988 (Unpublished report, NMRS MS/991/50/1–6).
3 Perry, 'Dunfermline', 788.
4 SUAT, Archive Report, 1988.
5 Perry, 'Dunfermline', 789.
6 Perry, 'Dunfermline', 788.
7 Perry, 'Dunfermline', 788.
8 FR Coles, 'Notices of rock-hewn caves in the Valley of the Esk and other parts of Scotland', *PSAS*, 45 (1910–11), 293–7.
9 Perry, 'Dunfermline', 788.
10 NMRS NT 08 NE 05.
11 Gourlay and Turner, *Historic Dunfermline* , 12; SUAT, *Historic Dunfermline*; Perry, 'Dunfermline', 785.
12 AAM Duncan, *Scotland The Making of A Kingdom* (Edinburgh, 1975), 472–3.
13 ACM Calder, Geophysical Investigation in Pittencrieff Park, Dunfermline, Fife (Unpublished Report 2001).
14 NMRS NT 08 NE 06.
15 Gifford, *Buildings*, 192. Henderson, *Annals*, argues for 1740.
16 1766 map.
17 Carnegie Dunfermline Trust Minutes, 1904, no 174.
18 Gifford, *Buildings*, 192.
19 Gifford, *Buildings*, 193, and shown on 1766 Map.
20 Gifford, *Buildings*, 192.
21 Gifford, Buildings, 192.
22 Chalmers, *Account*, i, 89–90.
23 Inventory of Historic Gardens and Designed Landscapes, Site No. 123, Fife.
24 Most recently EP Dennison, 'Living in Medieval Dunfermline', in *Royal Dunfermline*, ed. R Fawcett, 4–6.
25 NAS, B20/1/4, Protocol Book of Henry Elder, fo 25r (8 December 1657); fo 48v (3 December 1658), for example.
26 S Stronach, 'The medieval development of South Leith and the creation of Rotten Row', *PSAS*, 132 (2002), 383–423.
27 RM Spearman, 'The Medieval Townscape of Perth', in *The Scottish Medieval Town*, eds M Lynch, M Spearman and G Stell (Edinburgh, 1988), 42–59.
28 Spearman, 'Medieval Perth', 49–50.
29 SUAT, Monitoring of Environmental Improvements Works at Bridge Street/ Kirkgate/Maygate/St Catherines Wynd Dunfermline (unpublished Archive Report).
30 SUAT excavation archive, NMRS MS 991/49.
31 SUAT excavation archive, NMRS MS 991/49.
32 Coleman, 'Excavations', 70–112, in Fife Regional Council, *The Capital in the*

Kingdom, the Archaeology of Medieval Dunfermline (n.p. 1994), *passim.*
33 Coleman, 'Excavations', 74–5.
34 Coleman, 'Excavations', 108.
35 Coleman, 'Excavations', 74–5.
36 Coleman, 'Excavations', 108.
37 SUAT archive report, NMRS MS/991/53.
38 SUAT archive report, NMRS MS/991/53.
39 Gourlay and Turner, *Historic Dunfermline*, 11; R Cachart, '29–35 Bruce Street, Dunfermline, evaluation', *DES* (2003), 77.
40 Henderson, *Annals*, 619.
41 Henderson, *Annals*, 619.
42 *Dunfermline Press*, 24 December 1892.
43 SUAT, Evaluation and watching brief at 36–48 Bruce Street, Dunfermline (SUAT unpublished report, NMRS MS 1041/44).
44 Pitcairn, *History*, 161.
45 D Hall, Excavation in Dunfermline 1981 (SUAT unpublished report, NMRS MS 991/47/4).
46 Hall, Excavation.
47 Gourlay and Turner, *Historic Dunfermline.*
48 Perry, 'Dunfermline', 805.
49 Perry, 'Dunfermline', 805.
50 Gifford, *Buildings*, 188.
51 Perry, 'Dunfermline', 805.
52 EPD Torrie (ed.), *The Gild Court Book of Dunfermline 1433–1597* (Scottish Record Society, 1986), 166.
53 Perry, 'Dunfermline', 806.
54 Perry, 'Dunfermline', 806.
55 Perry, 'Dunfermline', 806.
56 B McEwan, pers comm.
57 EP Dennison, S Stronach and R Coleman, *Historic Dunbar: Archaeology and Development* (Scottish Burgh Survey, 2006), 80.
58 Coleman, 'Excavations', 107.
59 Henderson, *Annals*, 586.
60 Henderson, *Annals*, 590.
61 Henderson, *Annals*, 590.
62 B Robertson, pers comm.
63 *Contract of Copartnery of the East of Scotland Malleable Iron Co.*, published by J. Miller & Son, Dunfermline 1847.
64 *Dunfermline Advertiser*, 11 August 1848, quoted in Henderson *Annals*, 658.
65 Thomson, 'Anent Dunfermline', Vol.1, Item 225.
66 Henderson, *Annals*, 674.
67 Obituary of Mr Alexander Jackson from *Dunfermline Journal*, 30 September 1882.
68 Article in *Dunfermline Press*, 24 December 1892.
69 *Dunfermline Press*, report of September 1896.
70 *Dunfermline Press*, 24 December 1892.
71 *Dunfermline Press*, 28 August 1909; Walker, *Erskine Beveridge*, 64.
72 Thomson, *The Weavers Craft*, 337.
73 *Dunfermline Press*, 24 December 1892.
74 *Dunfermline Press*, 24 December 1892.
75 Much of the following information supplied in pers comm from M Watson.
76 Walker, *Dunfermline Linen*, 46.
77 Information supplementary to the Statutory List HB No. 26073.

78 Information supplementary to the Statutory List HB No. 26073.

79 Information supplementary to the Statutory List HB No. 26073.

80 Information supplementary to the Statutory List HB No. 26073; Walker, *Erskine Beveridge*, 64.

81 Walker, *Erskine Beveridge*, 64.

82 Wood 1823; Ordnance Survey 1896.

83 This and much of the following information from M Watson, pers comm.

84 Walker, *Erskine Beveridge*, 64.

85 Walker, *Erskine Beveridge*, 64.

86 Information supplementary to the Statutory List HB No. 46905.

87 Walker, *Erskine Beveridge*, 64.

88 Ordnance Survey 1896.

89 Walker, *Erskine Beveridge*, 64.

90 Information Supplementary to the Statutory List HB No. 46906; Walker, *Erskine Beveridge*, 64.

91 Walker, *Erskine Beveridge*, 64.

92 Walker, *Erskine Beveridge*, 64.

93 Information Supplementary to the Statutory List HB No. 46906.

94 Information Supplementary to the Statutory List HB No. 26041; Walker, *Erskine Beveridge*, 64.

95 Information Supplementary to the Statutory List HB No. 26041.

96 Gifford, *Buildings*, 193.

97 Henderson, *Viagraphia*, 40–1.

98 B McEwan, pers comm.

99 Lewis, 'Excavations', 1023–1044.

100 Lewis, 'Excavations', 1040.

101 Lewis, 'Excavations', 1040.

102 Lewis, 'Excavations', 1041.

103 As does the 1766 map.

104 Cowan and Easson (eds), *Religious Houses*, 175.

105 Perry, 'Dunfermline', 794.

106 T Robertson, 'St Leonard's', *DES* (1974), 83.

107 *NMRS* NT 08 NE 29.

108 *NMRS* NT 08 NE 30.

109 *NMRS* NT 08 NE 30.

110 *NMRS* MS/1244.

111 Taylor, 'Queen Margaret', 7–8.

112 Taylor, 'Queen Margaret', 7–8.

113 1766 Map.

114 For further discussion, *see* Taylor with Markus, *Place-Names*, 308–11.

115 Thomson, 'Anent Dunfermline', Item 14, Vol 9.

116 Thomson, 'Anent Dunfermline', Item 14, Vol 9.

117 *Dunfermline Press*, 10 September 1892.

118 M Watson, pers comm.

119 *Dunfermline Press*, 24 December 1892.

120 Henderson, *Annals*, 528; *Dunfermline Press*, 24 December 1892.

121 *Dunfermline Press*, 24 December 1892.

122 *Dunfermline Press*, 24 December 1892.

123 *Dunfermline Press*, 24 December 1892.

124 *Dunfermline Press*, 24 December 1892.

125 Walker, *Erskine Beveridge*, 64.

126 Walker, *Erskine Beveridge*, 64.

127 For an insight into the development of the works and the lives of people

associated with it *see* Walker, *Erskine Beveridge*.

128 Walker, *Erskine Beveridge*, 64.

129 *See* Simpson, *Auld Grey Toun*, 34 and 69–74 for further details.

130 Rev Dr J M Webster, *The Oldest Inhabited House in Dunfermline* (undated printed sheet in Dunfermline Library Local History Department).

131 Information Supplementary to the Statutory List HB No. 26044.

132 Gifford, *Buildings*.

133 Information Supplementary to the Statutory List HB No. 26022.

134 Information Supplementary to the Statutory List HB No. 1181.

135 S Pitcairn, pers comm.

136 For the most recent volume concerning the abbey *see Royal Dunfermline*, ed. R Fawcett.

137 R Fawcett, 'Dunfermline Abbey Church', in *Royal Dunfermline*, ed. R Fawcett, 27; NMRS Archive FID/89/22.

138 Fawcett, 'Church', 30–31.

139 Fawcett, 'Church', 33.

140 Fawcett, 'Church', 49.

141 *ER*, i, 215; N Bridgland, 'Dunfermline Abbey: Cloister and Precinct', in *Royal Dunfermline*, ed. Fawcett, 89.

142 Bridgland, 'Cloister', 96; TM Robertson, GH Williams, G Haggarty and N Reynolds, 'Recent excavations at Dunfermline Abbey, Fife' *PSAS*, 111 (1981), 388–400.

143 R Fawcett, Dunfermline Abbey: Historic Scotland Statement of Significance (Unpublished).

144 Hunt & Welwood, *Plan*.

145 Coleman, 'Excavations' and Lewis, 'Excavations'.

146 S Stronach and T Holden, Report of an Archaeological Assessment of 2–16 St Margaret Street and 1 Canmore Street, Dunfermline, Fife (Unpublished Headland Archive Report, 2003).

147 Lewis, 'Excavations', 1028.

148 Lewis, 'Excavations', 1028.

149 Coleman, 'Excavations', 76.

150 Dennison, 'Medieval Dunfermline', Figure 1.8.

151 Bridgland, 'Cloister', 98–9, and Bridgland also suggests that the northern line may have been marked only by a road.

152 Bridgland, 'Cloister', 98–9.

153 Information supplementary to the Statutory List HB No. 26028.

154 Bridgland, 'Cloister', 98–9.

155 Bridgland, 'Cloister', 98.

156 1766 Map.

157 Bridgland, 'Cloister', 96–7.

158 Coleman, 'Excavations', 74–5.

159 Coleman, 'Excavations', 74–5.

160 Coleman, 'Excavations', 81.

161 NMRS MS/991/52/1–10.

162 NMRS MS/991/52/1–10.

163 M Kimber, 14–16 St Margaret Street, Dunfermline, Fife: Data Structure Report of an Archaeological Excavation (Unpublished Headland Archaeology Archive Report, 2004).

164 Coleman, 'Excavations', 108–9.

165 Bridgland, 'Cloister', 99.

166 I Suddaby, *76* St Margaret Street, Dunfermline: Archaeological Investigations (Unpublished Centre for Field Archaeology Archive Report, 2001).

167 T Neighbour, '76 St Margaret Street, Dunfermline' *DES* 2000, 40; I Suddaby,

'76 St Margaret Street, Dunfermline', *DES* 2001, 46–7.

168 Dennison, 'Medieval Dunfermline', Figure 1.8.

169 Dennison, 'Medieval Dunfermline', Figure 1.8.

170 L Speed, An Archaeological Watching Brief at Monastery Street, Dunfermline, Fife (Unpublished Headland Archive Report, 1999).

171 R Coleman and S Stronach, An Archaeological Site Assessment at Buchanan Street Car Park, Dunfermline, Fife (Unpublished SUAT Archive Report, 1997).

172 Fawcett, 'Church', 56.

173 Fawcett, 'Church', 56.

174 Fawcett, 'Church', 57.

175 Fawcett, 'Church', 58–9.

176 A Barlow, 'Dunfermline Abbey', *DES* 1993, 27.

177 Hunt and Welwood, 1865 Map.

178 Walker, *Erskine Beveridge*, 64.

179 Walker, *Erskine Beveridge*, 64.

180 Walker, *Erskine Beveridge*, 64.

181 B McEwan, pers comm.

182 Thomas Pennant quoted in B.Skinner, 'The Heugh Mills at Dunfermline', *Scottish Studies*, Vol. 10, Part 2 (1966), 188–9.

183 Dennison, 'Medieval Dunfermline', Figure 1.8.

184 Skinner, 'Heugh Mills', Plate XII.

185 Skinner, 'Heugh Mills', 188.

186 Skinner, 'Heugh Mills', 189.

187 NMRS NT 08 NE 1.11 (although A MacKechnie 'The royal palace of Dunfermline', in *Royal Dunfermline*, ed. Fawcett, 101–38, compares this location to the King's Stables below Edinburgh and Stirling Castles.

A plan of the areas known to have archaeological potential is shown as **plate 10**.

Area 1: Pittencrieff Glen and west of Tower Burn

The area to the west of Tower Burn was part of Pittencrieff estate and quite distinct from both the abbey and burgh (*see* p 77). Consequently it has remained largely free of urban development and remains a fine designed landscape with Pittencrieff House at its heart. The area is listed on the Inventory of Historic Gardens and Designed Landscapes, which embraces both the landscape and the standing remains relating to the estate, such as the house itself and ancillary structures such as dovecots.

Archaeological remains relating to earlier phases of garden design are likely to survive. It has been noted that the place-name Pittencrieff contains the Pictish element *pett*, which refers to an estate farm.[1] This implies that an early settlement lies somewhere in the vicinity. The estate appears to have persisted into the medieval period and was recorded in the thirteenth century.[2] Presumably there was a corresponding medieval estate centre and the most obvious location would have been in the vicinity of Pittencrieff House.

As discussed in the previous chapter it has been suggested that an early medieval burgh was located in the Park. This possibility should not be ignored, but it should be noted that there have been no chance finds of medieval material to the west of Tower Burn and the historical reference that led to this hypothesis is difficult to interpret (*see* p 15).

Malcolm Canmore's Tower is protected as a Scheduled Ancient Monument and excavations have established that the visible foundations date to the fourteenth century. Much of the hillside around the monument has been faced with rock and while this work was being carried out it was noted that medieval middens survived. Presumably rubbish had been tipped over the edge of the summit when it was occupied. Any works around the hill should be archaeologically monitored to establish if pockets of midden still survive as this could produce more information on the nature of this, still rather enigmatic, monument.

Remains of lades, weirs and wells can be seen along the slopes of Pittencrieff Glen and beneath the surface of Tower Burn. Less obviously, there may be buried traces of past industries associated with the burgh or abbey along the burn's banks. In particular it was noted in the eighteenth century that the burgh inhabitants used the area to the north of Tower Hill for washing and bleaching (*see* p 41). The area around Tower Bridge may contain remains relating to its medieval predecessor.

Several caves with indications of early habitation have been found in the Glen (*see* p 78). It is possible that these were used as, not very isolated, hermitages by monks from the abbey or perhaps even earlier. Any further archaeological information on the date and nature of their use would be invaluable.

Area 2: north of the abbey precinct

The early burgh is thought to have been laid out along the north–south line of St Catherine's Wynd/Bruce Street and perpendicular to this along High Street. The original topography of the area seems to have been very important to the burgh's development. Most of the streets in the town run east to west along terraces that were presumably present naturally but have probably been exaggerated by later development. Preservation of archaeological deposits in the medieval town has been shown to vary in response to the underlying slope and the amount of later clearance.

Generally speaking, it seems that deposits to the north (upslope) are less well preserved because of extensive terracing into the slope in order to create level areas for development. However, even here, archaeological work has shown that medieval deposits and features can survive, and trial trenching should be carried out before any development. To the south it seems that several metres of deposits may have accumulated at the rear of High Street plots where midden and soil eroding down the slope have been piling up against the rear walls of properties so the archaeological potential is higher.

It is also worth pointing out that there is a significant slope at the west end of High Street, from the market cross toward Tower Burn. This may have been evened out over the years by the dumping of material prior to building work and preservation may be better at this end of High Street.

Although there is the potential for medieval remains to survive throughout this area there are several specific sites that may be identified. Beneath Bridge Street it is possible that structural remains relating to the town's earlier tolbooths survive. Traces of the town's ports may survive close to locations indicated in **figure 34** beneath the current roadway. Evidence for the mill that is known to have been located beside the Mill Port may survive in this area. The exact location of St Ninian's Chapel is not known but it may have been in the general vicinity indicated in **figure 34**. The medieval hospital documented in the vicinity of East Port may be located by excavation in this area. This region appears to have been a medieval suburb and excavation here should establish when the town spread outside the port in this direction. The discovery of a kiln, some two metres below the current ground surface at the corner of High Street and New Row, indicates that it is possible that a considerable depth of archaeological deposits survives in this area. It was recorded that a ditch was to be dug around the town on the orders of Edward I (*see* p 20). If effected, this deeply cut feature seems very likely to survive at least in part. Its location would define the extent of the town in the fourteenth century, and it may have filled with midden deposits that would tell us much about life in the town.

The area to the north of High Street was the most important in terms of the town's industrial development. Many industrial buildings were still standing (at least in part) at the time of the survey but it seems likely that they will be subject to redevelopment soon. Historic building recording of these industrial structures can reveal much about their development, layout and function; and also the social hierarchies that existed when they functioned. This is fundamental and imperative as a mechanism to capture Dunfermline's past. It would also provide an invaluable record for the future. It is important that any developments associated with these are accompanied by planning conditions that allow for their adequate recording and interpretation before they are lost forever. Even where buildings have been demolished remains relating to them can survive as sub-surface remains, notably water courses, culverts, sluices, cooling ponds, wells, engine bases, condensers and power transmission systems that may have been below floors. These can be excavated and recorded to provide information concerning the town's important industrial heritage, which is every bit as important as its medieval roots.

Area 3: New Row and Netherton

The archaeological potential of properties lining New Row has been established by excavation. Although much modern development has occurred along this street, medieval remains may still be preserved. The potential seems higher to the south of the street, where the previous excavations were located, and less modern development has occurred. It should not be assumed, however, that remains do not survive beneath modern development between Canmore Street and High Street.

The only excavations to be undertaken in the vicinity of Netherton were those in the graveyard of St Leonard's Hospital. No excavations have been undertaken within the area of medieval and post-medieval development. Much modern development has occurred along the line of the medieval street, but it should not be assumed that this has removed all earlier remains. As discussed earlier, it is possible that Netherton developed in tandem with High Street and it is important to establish the date of earliest settlement in this area. Ground floor and basement hand-loom shops existed in the area (one of them, a social club at the time of writing, is still visible) and are likely to be cut into the hillside.[3] They had earthen floors to maintain a level of humidity that would reduce breakage of warp threads.

In addition, there are several important sites within Netherton that deserve closer inspection. Lady's Mill at the west end of Broad Street was recorded in the medieval period. Although modern development now covers the area it once stood in, it is possible that remains survive, especially those associated with deeply cut features such as a lade. St Mary's Chapel stood in the vicinity of Elgin Street, and remains of it and those relating to St Leonard's Hospital may still survive.

In addition to the medieval and post-medieval potential of Netherton it is possible that the earliest origins of Dunfermline lie within this area. As has been discussed (*see* p 15), there are some indications that Perdieus Mount may be in the vicinity of an earlier settlement. The whole area of the confluence of Tower and Lyne Burns should be regarded as archaeologically sensitive.

Area 4: the abbey precinct

Part of the abbey is a Scheduled Ancient Monument but this is too narrow a focus to understand its full extent. Everything within the precinct should be regarded as belonging to a nationally important site including parts since absorbed by the town. The possible limits of the precinct are shown in **figures 34 and 35**. Archaeological excavations have recorded remains surviving throughout the precinct and it seems that preservation of deposits and structures is generally excellent. In addition, some waterlogged features have been noted. Waterlogging is very important archaeologically as it allows preservation of organic artefacts made out of materials like leather and wood that are rarely found on excavation. Any excavations have the potential to contain evidence relating to the abbey precinct and also any earlier ecclesiastical site that may have existed here.

It was noted that the ruins of Heugh Mills were surviving to a height of up to 20 feet (over six metres) in 1966.[4] If this figure was accurate, an alarming amount of degradation has occurred over the last 40 years, as today the walls are closer to a height of three metres. In addition to weathering, the walls are being made less stable by vegetation, including tree growth. The substantial roots growing between the stones will make short work of any remaining lime mortar.

Structural stability is also a concern with St Catherine's Almshouse, which has several mature trees growing out of its roof. If this vegetation growth is allowed to continue and no consolidation work is carried out, it can only be a matter of time before these nationally important monuments are reduced to rubble. However, consolidation is a delicate matter and should be informed by a thorough understanding of the way that the structure was built and performs.

Any ground disturbance within the precinct should be accompanied by archaeological mitigation. In addition, it has been noted that some of the post-medieval standing buildings are probably eighteenth-century in date. The building at no 92 St Margaret Street **figure 34** is currently uninhabited and archaeological recording could reveal much about it and its inhabitants' histories. It is also apparent that many of the standing walls, such as those around the car park on Buchanan Street, are likely to be early post-medieval in date. These enhance the historic atmosphere of the area, and their positions and sequence of construction could contain information relating to the development of the precinct immediately after the demise of the monastery. It is also possible that some of these walls had origins as medieval boundaries.

The precinct wall survives in part and has been designated a Scheduled Ancient Monument for a small part of its circuit. Excavation has shown it also survives below the ground elsewhere.[5] It also survives above ground, and is still accessible at the time of survey, on the east side of the buildings at the corner of Canmore Street and St Margaret Street, one formerly the St Margaret Hotel **figure 34**.[6] On the south side of the precinct it is possible that parts of a surviving wall, marked as the site or part of Palace Wall on the Ordnance Survey plan surveyed in 1855, are also surviving remnants of the precinct wall. In particular, the stretch over the lade, and enclosing Heugh Mills on the south and west, looks wider at its base, which is a typically medieval feature. Certainly, it is similar to the surviving remnant at Canmore Street.

Future research

Archaeological mitigation in order to record threatened remains and inform development decisions should be a consideration before ground disturbance work in the burgh, and particularly in the areas of focus in this book **plate 10**. The early history and development of the settlement is poorly understood and can be illuminated only by further archaeological excavation. The results of excavations will provide material for further research into the town's development, and into the daily lives of the inhabitants. It is important that this work includes not only High Street but also New Row and Netherton.

The standing remains relating to both Heugh Mills and St Catherine's almshouse are nationally important. The survival of both is threatened by a lack of management. It is important that the remaining features and condition of these significant and rare survivals be recorded before any further information is lost. This should also provide information as to how best to manage these remains. As standing structures that can be readily understood by members of the public, the current lack of interpretation at both sites is perhaps a missed opportunity to spread a greater understanding of key features of Dunfermline's past. Promoting access would, of course, depend on considerations of public safety as well as the condition of the monuments.

The layout of the abbey precinct is poorly understood and much of it lies outside the area protected as a Scheduled Ancient Monument. It is important that archaeological excavation of all deposits and structures threatened with disturbance is undertaken. In this way we should increase our knowledge of one of Scotland's most important monasteries.

The development of mills and factories is often an overlooked part of archaeology, but of equal importance to understanding the medieval past. The town's historic mills and factories are disappearing and efforts should be undertaken to record these in order to better understand the town's post-medieval development and industrial revolution hey-day. For example, the transition from hand to powered manufacturing was by no means straightforward, as is demonstrated in the case of Dunfermline's linen industry (*see* p 61).

The Dunfermline Museum has a collection of material, including pot and bone that has been collected from in and around the town. Further examination of this material will be very worthwhile where related to specific sites.

Dunfermline has a rich history and archaeology, which would be the envy of many other historic towns. Still more care than has been exercised in the past should be taken to protect its historic and archaeological future. The people of Dunfermline, of the present generation and those to come, deserve no less.

Notes

1 Taylor, 'Welcome to Fothrif'.
2 Perry, 'Dunfermline', 806.
3 M Watson, pers comm.
4 Skinner, 'Heugh Mills', 189.
5 Lewis, 'Excavations'.
6 Stronach and Holden, 'Report'.

Glossary of technical terms

aerial photography	Identifying and recording sites that are not clearly apparent on the ground from the air. For example, sites can become obvious because of shadows in low light and especially through cropmarks (*see* below).
almshouse	A house founded by charity and dedicated to helping the poor.
Anglo-Saxons	People who settled in Britain from the Low Countries and Germany in the fifth or sixth centuries. They are also described as Angles and Anglian.
artefacts	Objects made by human workmanship.
backland	The area to the rear of the burgage plot behind the dwelling house on the frontage. Originally intended for growing produce and keeping animals; site of wells and midden heaps. Eventually housed working premises of craftsmen and poorer members of burgh society.
bailies	Burgh officers who performed routine administration.
boundaries	*see* burgage plot
Bronze Age	The prehistoric period between the Neolithic and the Iron Age (*see* below) or around 2,000–500 BC. Named because of the introduction of bronze working.
building recording	A specialised branch of archaeology involving the analysis, recording and interpretation of buildings.
burgage plot	A division of land, often of regular size, having been measured out by liners, allocated to a burgess. Once built on, it contained the burgage house on the frontage (*see* frontage) and a backland (*see* backland). In time, with pressure for space, the plots were often subdivided (*see* repletion). Plots were bounded by ditches, wattle fences or stone walls.
burgess	Person who enjoyed the privileges and responsibilities of the freedom of the burgh.
Canmore	A computerised database maintained by RCHAMS. Covers the whole of Scotland and contains information on many standing buildings, chance finds and archaeological works.

Carboniferous	A geological period extending from around 359 million years ago to around 299 million years ago, named because of the extensive coal beds of this age in Western Europe.
cist	A stone-lined grave; two types are common (*see* short cist and long cist) although variations occur.
cloister	Enclosed court attached to a monastery and comprising a roofed walkway around an open area.
close	*see* vennel
craft	Trade.
cropmarks	Crops growing over archaeological sites and indicating the presence of buried features such as walls and ditches because of differing rates of ripening.
damask	Woven fabric (usually silk or linen) with a pattern visible on both sides.
Dark Age	The period between the collapse of the western Roman Empire and the establishment of the feudal medieval system, around AD 400–1,000.
documentary sources	Written evidence, primary sources being the original documents.
evaluation	A programme of site investigations often comprising desk-based research, trial trenching, and building recording.
excavation	The controlled removal and recording of archaeological deposits; often following an evaluation (*see* above) which has established their presence.
façade	Finished face of a building.
finds	A term used to refer to artefacts but also including food waste, for example seeds and bones.
frater	*see* refectory
frontage	Front part of burgage plot nearest the street, on which the dwelling was usually built.
guild	Organisation or fraternity for mutual support, whether economic, religious or social.

hinterland	Rural area around a burgh, to which the burgh looked for economic and agricultural support; hinterland likewise dependent on burgh market.
Iron Age	The final prehistoric period in Britain named because of the introduction of iron working. Running from around 500 BC – AD 500, although the latter half is often termed the Roman Iron Age.
lade	Artificial channel created to carry water.
midden	Used by archaeologists to describe soils thought to have accumulated through the disposal of domestic waste, although through the processes of decay much of the waste will not have survived except for durable items, especially fragments of pottery.
mortify	To bequeath to a charitable institution.
motte	An earthen mound topped by a castle, usually associated with a bailey (an enclosure), and introduced into Britain by the Normans.
Neolithic	The prehistoric period beginning with the introduction of farming around 4,000 BC until the Bronze Age, around 2,000 BC.
Picts	The British (*see* above) tribe occupying northern Scotland.
pillory	Wooden frame with holes for restraining a person to be subject to public humiliation.
post-medieval	The period from the sixteenth to eighteenth century.
precinct	Enclosed space.
prehistory	The period of human history before the advent of writing.
refectory	Dining hall of a monastery.
repletion	*see* burgage plot
rig	*see* burgage plot
Scheduled Ancient Monument	Scheduled Ancient Monument A monument protected under the terms of the Ancient Monuments and Archaeological Areas Act 1979.
solar	Medieval chamber or room.

souterrain	The name given by archaeologists to a type of underground structure with the form of a passageway lined with stone slabs and built in the late Iron Age.
spindle whorl	A doughnut-shaped object used as a weight during spinning.
subsoil	Usually taken to mean a layer of clay, silt or sand beneath topsoil (*see* below) and deposits made by people such as midden (*see* above). In most parts of Scotland this comprises undisturbed glacial deposits and may also be called 'natural'.
toft	*see* burgage plot
tolbooth	The most important secular building; meeting place of burgh council; collection post for market tolls; often housed town gaol.
tolls	Payments for use of burgh market.
topography	The physical characteristics of land.
town-house	Principal modern civic building.
tron	Public weigh-beam.
vennel	Alley; narrow lane.
vernacular buildings	Unpretentious traditional structures.
watching brief	The archaeological monitoring of excavation works conducted by others.

1 Manuscript sources

Guildry of Dunfermline

MS Guild Merchant records, 1586–1770

National Archives of Scotland

B20/1/1 Protocol Book of John Cunninghame, 1556/7–1576
B20/1/2 Protocol Book of David Brown, 1594–1612
B20/1/3 Protocol Book of Johne Auchinwallis, 1642–50
B20/1/4 Protocol Book of Henry Elder, 1656–61
B20/13/2–15 Dunfermline Burgh Council Minutes, 1662–1812
CH2/592/1–5 Dunfermline Kirk Session Records, 1640–1734
E69/10/1 Hearth Tax, Dunfermline, 1691
E326/1/42 Window Tax, Fife County, 1748
RH2/1/76 Protocol Book of John Cunynghame, 1556/7–76
    (transcript of B20/1/1)
RH11/27/15–17 Dunfermline Regality, Register of Decreets,
    1591–1636
RH11/27/18–19 Dunfermline Regality Court Book, 1612–80

National Library of Scotland

Adv. Ms. 29.4.2 (vi) 'Hutton's Collections', vol. vi, Linlithgow, Stirling,
    Kinross, Fife.
'Annual Reports of the Inspectors of Mines', in *Reports from
    Commissioners, Inspectors and Others to Parliament, 1876* (PP, xvii)

2 Printed primary sources

Accounts of the Master of Works, eds HM Paton *et al* (Edinburgh, 1957–)
Accounts of the Lord High Treasurer of Scotland, eds T Dickson *et al*,
    (Edinburgh, 1877–1916)
The Acts of the Parliaments of Scotland, eds T Thomson and C Innes
    (Edinburgh, 1814–75)
Androw of Wyntoun, the Orygynale Cronykil of Scotland, ed. D Laing
    (*The Historians of Scotland*, ii, Edinburgh, 1872–9)
Beveridge, E (ed.), *The Burgh Records of Dunfermline* (Edinburgh, 1917)
Calderwood, D, *The History of the Kirk of Scotland* (Wodrow Soc., 1842–9)
Calendar of Documents relating to Scotland, ed. J Bain (Edinburgh, 1881–8)

Calendar of Entries in the Papal Registers relating to Great Britain and Ireland: Papal Letters, ed. JM Tremlow (London, 1933)

Calendar of Scottish Supplications to Rome, eds J Kirk, RJ Tanner and AI Dunlop (Edinburgh, 1997)

The Charters of King David I: the Written Acts of David I King of Scots, 1124–53, and of his Son Henry Earl of Northumberland, 1139–52, ed. GWS Barrow (Woodbridge, 1999)

Contract of Copartnery of the East of Scotland Malleable Iron Co. (Dunfermline, 1847)

Cowan, IB, and Easson, DE (eds), *Medieval Religious Houses. Scotland* (Glasgow, 1976)

Dennison, EP, 'Dunfermline gild court book: missing folios', *Miscellany XIII* (SHS, 2004)

[Dennison] Torrie, EPD (ed.), *The Gild Court Book of Dunfermline, 1433–1597* (SRS, 1986)

Dickinson, WC (ed.), *John Knox's History of the Reformation in Scotland*, 2 vols (London, 1949)

Froissart, J, *Chronicles of England, France, Spain, Portugal, Brittany, Flanders and the adjoining countries* (London, 1812)

Heron, R, *Scotland Delineated* (Edinburgh, 1797; reprinted Edinburgh, 1975)

Johannis de Fordun, Chronica Gentis Scotorum, ed. WF Skene (Edinburgh, 1871–2)

Pennant, T, *A Tour in Scotland, and Voyage to the Hebrides* (Chester, 1774; reprint Edinburgh, 1998)

Pococke, R, *Tours in Scotland, 1747, 1750, 1760* (SHS, 1887)

'Register containing the State and Condition of Every Burgh within the Kingdom of Scotland, in the Year 1692', in *Miscellany of the Scottish Burgh Records Society* (Edinburgh, 1881)

The Register of the Privy Council of Scotland, eds JH Burton *et al* (Edinburgh, 1877–)

Registrum de Dunfermlyn (Bannatyne Club, 1842)

Registrum Magnii Sigilli Regum Scotorum, eds JM Thomson *et al* (Edinburgh, 1882–1914)

Registrum Secreti Sigilli Regum Scotorum, eds M Livingstone *et al* (Edinburgh, 1908–)

Shearer, A, *Extracts from the Burgh Records of Dunfermline in the Sixteenth and Seventeenth Centuries* (Dunfermline,1951)

The Statistical Account of Scotland, 1791–1799, ed. Sir John Sinclair (Wakefield, 1973)

Watt, DER, and Shead, N (eds), *The Heads of Religious Houses in Scotland from Twelfth to Fifteenth Centuries* (SRS, 2001)

3 Printed secondary sources

Barlow, A, 'Dunfermline Abbey', *DES* (1993)

Barr, WT, *For a Web Begun; the Story of Dunfermline* (Edinburgh, 1947)

Beveridge, E, *Viagraphia Dunfermlynensis* (Dunfermline, 1827; rev. edn, 1858)

Boardman, S, 'Dunfermline as a royal mausoleum', in R Fawcett (ed.), *Royal Dunfermline* (Edinburgh, 2005)

Bridgland, N, 'Dunfermline Abbey: cloister and precinct', in R Fawcett (ed.), *Royal Dunfermline* (Edinburgh, 2005)

Brotchie, A, *Wheels Around Dunfermline and Fife* (Catrine, n.d.)

Brotchie, A, and Jack, H, *The Early Railways of Fife* (forthcoming, 2007).

Cachart, R, '29–35 Bruce Street, Dunfermline, evaluation', *DES* (2003)

Callander, JG, and Bryce, TH, 'Bronze Age short cists near Dunfermline, Fife. With a report on the bones found', *PSAS*, lvii *(1922–3)*

Chalmers, P, *Historical and Statistical Account of Dunfermline* (Edinburgh, 1884)

Close-Brooks, J *et al*, 'A Bronze Age cemetery at Aberdour Road, Dunfermline, Fife', *PSAS*, civ *(1971–2)*

Coleman, R, 'Excavations at the Abbot's House, Maygate, Dunfermline', *TAFAJ*, 2 *(1996)*

Coles, FR, 'Notices of rock-hewn caves in the valley of the Esk and other parts of Scotland', *PSAS*, xlv (1910–11)

Cunningham, AS, *Romantic Culross, Torryburn, Carnock, Cairneyhill, Saline and Pitfirrane* (Dunfermline, 1902)

Dennison, EP, 'Living in medieval Dunfermline' in R Fawcett (ed.), *Royal Dunfermline* (Edinburgh, 2005)

Dennison, EP, 'Medieval burghs' in D Omand (ed.), *The Fife Book* (Edinburgh, 2000)

Dennison, EP, and Coleman, R, *Historic Linlithgow* (Scottish Burgh Survey, 2000)

Dennison, EP, and Coleman, R, *Historic Musselburgh* (Scottish Burgh Survey, 1996)

Dennison, EP, Stronach, S, and Coleman, R, *Historic Dunbar* (Scottish Burgh Survey, 2006)

Dilworth, M, 'Dunfermline, Duries and the Reformation', *Records of the Scottish Church History Society*, 31 (2002)

Dilworth, M, 'Monks and ministers after 1560', *Records of the Scottish Church History Society*, 18 (1974)

Duncan, AAM, *Scotland: The Making of the Kingdom* (Edinburgh, 1975)

Dunfermline City Trail (Dunfermline, n.d.)

Fawcett, R, *The Abbey and Palace of Dunfermline* (Historic Scotland, 1990)

Fawcett, R, 'Dunfermline Abbey Church', in R Fawcett (ed.), *Royal Dunfermline* (Edinburgh, 2005)

Fawcett, R, *Medieval Abbeys and Churches of Fife: a Heritage Guide* (Fife Regional Council, n.d.)

Fawcett, R (ed.), *Royal Dunfermline* (Edinburgh, 2005)

Fergusson, J, *The White Hind and Other Discoveries* (London, 1963)

Fernie, J, *A History of the Town and Parish of Dunfermline* (Dunfermline, 1815)

Fife Regional Council, *The Capital in the Kingdom: the Archaeology of Medieval Dunfermline* (n.p., 1994)

Geddes, Sir P, *City Development. A Study of Parks, Gardens and Culture-Institutes: a Report to the Carnegie Dunfermline Trust* (Dunfermline, 1904)

Gifford, J, *The Buildings of Scotland: Fife* (London, 1988)

Gillen, C, 'Rocks and Landscapes', in D Omand (ed.), *The Fife Book* (Edinburgh, 2000)

Gourlay, R, and Turner, A, *Historic Dunfermline; the Archaeological Implications of Development* (Scottish Burgh Survey, 1978)

Grant, J, *History of the Burgh Schools of Scotland* (London and Glasgow, 1876)

Grose, F, *The Antiquities of Scotland*, 2 vols (London, 1797)

Henderson, E, *Annals of Dunfermline and Vicinity* (Glasgow, 1879)

Hunter, TF, *Mining in West Fife: the Crossgates Area, in particular Fordell and Halbeath Collieries* (Norwich, 2001)

Historic Scotland, *Memorandum of Guidance on Listed Buildings and Conservation Areas* (1998)

Keay, J, and Keay, J, *Collins Encyclopaedia of Scotland* (London, 1994)

Lewis, J, 'Excavations at the former Lauder Technical College, Dunfermline', *PSAS*, cxxv (1995)

McEwan, B, *Dunfermline: Our Heritage* (Dunfermline, 1998)

Marshall, DN, 'Carved stone balls', *PSAS*, cviii (1976–7)

Maxwell, GS, and Ritchie, JNG, 'Prehistoric, Roman and Pictish Fife', in J Gifford (ed.), *The Buildings of Scotland: Fife* (London, 1988)

Mercer, A, *The History of Dunfermline from the Earliest Records down to the Present Time* (Dunfermline, 1828)

Naismith, RJ, *Buildings of the Scottish Countryside* (London, 1985)

Neighbour, T, '76 St. Margaret Street, Dunfermline', *DES* (2000)

Oglethorpe, M, *Scottish Collieries: an Inventory of Scotland's Coal Industry in the Nationalised Era* (Edinburgh, 2006)

Perry, D, 'Dunfermline: from "Saracen" castle to "populous manufacturing royal burrow"', *PSAS*, cxxxix (1999)

Pitcairn, S, *Dunfermline Abbey and Churchyard* (Edinburgh, 2003)

Pitcairn, S, *A History of The Old 'Fitpaths' and Streets of Dunfermline, Then and Now* (Dunfermline, n.d.)

Pride, G, *The Kingdom of Fife: An Illustrated Architectural Guide* (Royal Incorporation of Architects in Scotland, 1990)

Proudfoot, E, 'Living with the Romans', in D Omand (ed.), *The Fife Book* (Edinburgh, 2000)

Robertson, T, 'St Leonards', *DES* (1974)

Robertson, TM, Williams, GH, Haggarty, G, and Reynolds, N, 'Recent excavations at Dunfermline Abbey, Fife', *PSAS*, cxi (1981)

Royal Dunfermline: a City Awakening (Prospectus of the 'Royal Dunfermline' project, n.d.)

Scottish Natural Heritage, *Inventory of Gardens and Designed Landscapes in Scotland*, vol. 3, *Fife* (Edinburgh, 2005)

Simpson, E, *The Auld Grey Toun* (Dunfermline, 1987)

Skinner, B, 'The Heugh Mills at Dunfermline', *Scottish Studies*, 10 (1966)

Somerville, R, *Dunfermline Sketches and Notes* (Dunfermline, 1917)

Spearman, RM, 'The medieval townscape of Perth', in M Lynch, M Spearman and G Stell (eds), *The Scottish Medieval Town* (Edinburgh, 1988)

Stewart, A, *Reminiscences of Dunfermline* (Dunfermline, 1886)

Stronach, S, 'The medieval development of South Leith and the creation of Rotten Row', *PSAS*, cxxxii (2002)

SUAT, *Historic Dunfermline; the Archaeological Implications of Development* (Scottish Burgh Survey Update, 1998)

Suddaby, I, '76 St.Margaret Street, Dunfermline', *DES* (2001)

Taylor, JJ, *Bronze Age Goldwork of the British Isles* (Cambridge, 1980)

Taylor, S, 'Place-names of Fife', in D Omand (ed.), *The Fife Book* (Edinburgh, 2000)

Taylor, S, with Markus, G, *The Place-Names of Fife: Volume 1 West Fife between Leven and Forth* (Donington, 2006)

Taylor, S, 'Some early Scottish place-names and Queen Margaret', *Scottish Language*, xiii (1994)

Taylor, S, 'Welcome to Fothrif', *Scottish Place Name Society Newsletter*, xiii (Autumn, 2002)

Thomson, D, *The Dunfermline Hammermen: a History of the Incorporation of Hammermen in Dunfermline* (Paisley, 1909)

Thomson, D, *The Weavers' Craft, being a History of the Weavers' Incorporation of Dunfermline* (Paisley, 1903)

Walker, H, *Dunfermline Linen: The History of Hay and Robertson Ltd and the Robertson Family of Dunfermline* (Dunfermline, 1996)

Walker, H, *The Story of Erskine Beveridge and St Leonard's Works, 1833–1989* (Dunfermline, 1991)

Warden, AJ, *The Linen Trade, Ancient and Modern* (London, 1864)

Whittow, JB, *Geology and Scenery in Scotland* (London, 1977)

Wilkie, J, *Bygone Fife* (Edinburgh, 1931)

Wormald, J, *Court, Kirk and Community: Scotland 1470–1625* (London, 1981)

4 Newspapers

Dunfermline Advertiser
Dunfermline Journal
Dunfermline Press
Dunfermline Saturday Press and West of Fife Advertiser

5 Cartographic sources

1642 'Fifeshire' by James Gordon
1654 *Atlas of Scotland, West Fife* by Johannes Blaeu
1745 'Shires of Fife & Kinross' by Herman Moll
1747–55 'Military Survey of Scotland' by W. Roy, British Library
    Shelfmark: Maps C.9.b.17.10/1.
1766 'A View of the Town of Dunfermline, with the situation and
    distance of the [—] from the said town, surveyed and delineated
    in the year 1766 by [—]' (Dunfermline Carnegie Library)
1771 'The Estate of Pittencrief, Luscar & Clune' (NAS, RHP199)
1775 *County of Fife* by John Ainslie
1823 Wood, J. *Plan of the Town of Dunfermline*, scale 1:264
1823 'Boundaries report 1823' (Dunfermline Carnegie Library)
1827 *Atlas of Scotland, Fife & Kinross*
1828 *Fife & Kinross*
1829 'Plan of the town and lands of Dunfermline' (Dunfermline
    Carnegie Library)
1836 'Plan of Heugh Mills of Dunfermline with Mill Dams & Mill
    Lades belonging therein' (Dunfermline Carnegie Library)
1837 *Ordnance Survey, Dunfermline Town Plan*
1838 'Dunfermline Town & Parish Plan' (Dunfermline Carnegie
    Library)
1853 'Dunfermline Boundary Map' (Dunfermline Carnegie Library)
1855 'Plan of Dunfermline Abbey and neighbouring property
    showing ground in dispute *in causa* Lord Advocate v. Hunt of
    Pittencrieff' (NAS, RHP1686)
1856 *Ordnance Survey, Town Plan of Dunfermline*, sheets 1–7; scale 1:1056
1896 *Ordnance Survey, Town Plan of Dunfermline*, sheets xxxvii, xxxix;
    scale 1:500
1898–1904 *Ordnance Survey*, 1st series, 2nd edition, sheet 40
1912 *Survey Atlas of Scotland* (Edinburgh)
1928 *Geological Survey of Scotland* (1928), 'Fifeshire Western Division',
    sheet xxxviii
1952 'Map of XVIth century Dunfermline' by JR (Dunfermline
    Carnegie Library)
2000 Dunfermline Rectified AP, scale 1:1,000 (Fife Council
    Development Services, Archaeological Unit)

2001 *Ordnance Survey Explorer,* sheet *367* 1:25000
2005 *Dunfermline Street Map* (Dunfermline)

Undated

'Dunfermline Riggs', Fife Council Development Services,
    Archaeological Unit, 1:500
'Lands south of Netherton' (Archives of the Earl of Elgin and
    Kincardine, temporary reference 46/278)
'Listed buildings in Central Dunfermline', Fife Council Development
    Services, Archaeological Unit, 1:3000
'Listed buildings in Central Dunfermline', Fife Council Development
    Services, Archaeological Unit, 1:6000
'Street map of Dunfermline in Fife in year 1500' (Dunfermline
    Carnegie Library)
Street Plan of Dunfermline, by AW Bell (Dunfermline Press)

6 Unpublished sources

Calder, ACM, 'Geophysical Investigation in Pittencrieff Park,
    Dunfermline, Fife' (2001)
Carnegie Dunfermline Trust Minutes (1904)
Coleman, R, and Stronach, S, 'An Archaeological Site Assessment
    at Buchanan Street Car Park, Dunfermline, Fife' (SUAT Archive
    Report, 1997)
'Dunfermline Abbey: remains of first church *c.*1070' (NMRS, FID/
    89/22)
Hall, D, 'Excavation in City Bakery, Dunfermline 1981' (SUAT Archive
    Report, NMRS MS 991/47/4)
Historic Scotland, Information Supplementary to the Statutory List
    HB No. 1181, 26022, 26028, 26041, 26044, 26073, 46905, 46906'
    (online via Pastmap)
Kimber, M, '14–16 St Margaret Street, Dunfermline, Fife: Data
    Structure Report of an Archaeological Excavation 2004'
    (Headland Archaeology Archive Report, 2004)
'The Lord Appellant against James Hunt, Respondent' (Dunfermline
    Carnegie Library)
McEwan, B, 'Closes' (typescript, 2006)
Masterton, J, 'A study of growth patterns and changing cultural
    landscapes of a Scottish town' (typescript, Dunfermline Carnegie
    Library)
Millar, RT, 'Water supply: a short historical note' (typescript, 1966,
    Dunfermline Carnegie Library)
Millennium Project, 'Twentieth Century Dunfermline'

Shearer, A, 'Notes on Minute Book for the Dean of Guild Court of Dunfermline, begun 20 February 1753 and ending 15 July 1778' (Dunfermline Carnegie Library)

Speed, L, 'An archaeological watching brief at Monastery Street, Dunfermline, Fife' (Headland Archaeology Archive Report, 1999)

Stronach, S, and Holden, T, 'Report of an Archaeological Assessment of 2–16 St Margaret Street and 1 Canmore Street, Dunfermline, Fife 2003' (Headland Archaeology Archive Report, 2003)

SUAT, 'Abbot Street, Library, Dunfermline' (SUAT Archive Report, NMRS MS/991/52/1–10)

SUAT, 'Evaluation and watching brief at 36–48 Bruce Street, Dunfermline' (SUAT Archive Report, NMRS MS 1041/44)

SUAT, 'High Street Pedestrianisation, Dunfermline' (SUAT Archive Report, NMRS MS 991/53 /1–5)

SUAT, 'Malcolm Canmore's Tower, Dunfermline' (SUAT Archive Report, 1988, NMRS MS/991/50/1–6)

SUAT, 'Monitoring of Environmental Improvements Works at Bridge Street/Kirkgate/Maygate/St Catherine's Wynd, Dunfermline' (SUAT Archive Report)

SUAT, 'Wilson's Close, Dunfermline' (SUAT Archive Report, NMRS MS 991/49)

Suddaby, I, '76 St. Margaret Street, Dunfermline: Archaeological Investigations 2001' (CFA Archive Report, 2001; NMRS MS 1081/49)

Thomson, D, 'Anent Dunfermline, Manuscript Notes, Antiquarian and Contemporary' (Dunfermline Carnegie Library)

Torrie, EP Dennison, 'The Gild of Dunfermline in the Fifteenth Century' (Ph.D., University of Edinburgh, 1984)

'Unpublished report on archaeological watching brief at Perdieus Mount 1995' (NMRS MS/1244)

Watt, R, 'History of coal mining round Dunfermline' (typescript, 1999, Dunfermline Carnegie Library)

Webster, JM, 'The lands of Baldridge' (typescript, Dunfermline Carnegie Library)

Webster, JM, 'The lands of Masterton', in 'Notes on the burgh of Dunfermline' (typescript, Dunfermline Carnegie Library)

Webster, JM, 'Notes on the burgh of Dunfermline' (typescript, Dunfermline Carnegie Library)

Webster, JM, 'The oldest inhabited house in Dunfermline' (undated sheet, Dunfermline Carnegie Library)

NMRS NT 08 NE 01	Dunfermline Abbey
NMRS NT 08 NE 01.10	Dunfermline Abbey, Mill
NMRS NT 08 NE 01.11	Dunfermline Abbey, Kings Barns and Stables
NMRS NT 08 NE 0	Dunfermline, Pittencrieff Park, Malcolm Canmore's Tower
NMRS NT 08 NE 05	Dunfermline, Wallace Spa Well
NMRS NT 08 NE 06	Dunfermline, Pittencrieff Park, Pittencrieff House
NMRS NT 08 NE 08	Dunfermline, St Catherine's Chapel
NMRS NT 08 NE 14	Dunfermline, Gold Torc
NMRS NT 08 NE 22	Craigs Farm, Cairn
NMRS NT 08 NE 29	Dunfermline, St Mary's Chapel
NMRS NT 08 NE 30	Dunfermline, Perdieus Mount
NMRS NT 08 NE 36	Crossford, Keavil House Estate, Cist, Food Vessel
NMRS NT 08 NE 37	Wellwood, Flanged, Bronze Axe
NMRS NT 08 NE 38	Langlees, Glenmoy, Enclosure
NMRS NT 08 NE 83	Dunfermline, 63 Woodmill Street
NMRS NT 08 NE 94	Dunfermline, Pittencrieff Park, Heugh Mills
NMRS NT 08 SW 17	Pitreavie House, Stone Axe
NMRS NT 18 NW 4	Dunfermline, Easter Pitcorthie, Standing Stone
NMRS NT 18 NW 12	North Wood, Dunfermline, Cairn
NMRS NT 18 NW 25	Deanpark House, Mortuary Enclosure (Possible)
NMRS NT 18 SW 14	Middlebank, Urns
NMRS NT 18 SW 33	Masterton, Cist, Jet Necklace, Bronze Dagger
NMRS NT 18 SW 116	Middlebank, Souterrain (Possible)

Dovecoat